A Gal Growing Up Green Creek

A Collection of Memories of Farm Life in the Midwest

A Gal Growing Up Green Creek

A Collection of Memories of Farm Life in the Midwest

Anita C. Deters

All Rights Reserved.

No part of this publication may be reproduced in any form or by any means, including scanning, photocopying, or otherwise without prior written permission of the copyright holder.

Printed in the United Stated
Copyright © 2025 Anita C. Deters

ISBN-13: 978-1-944662-91-2

Cover Art Design
by Diana Henderson

Dedication

To all my nieces, nephews, great-nieces, and great-nephews and their children. It is important to keep the German legacy alive, not?

To all my girlfriends in the neighborhood where I grew up in Green Creek, in particular my cousins Cindy Niebrugge Darst and Marilyn Niebrugge Vohs. The giggles I shared with the two of you created a lasting memory! Of course, every playdate with my friend from across the field, Linda Ungrund Schumacher, was a treat!

To my cousin from Chicago, Sharon Deters Rodriguez. I always looked forward to your annual summer visit! I am delighted my family made an impression on you including my dad's rushed prayers over a family meal and Mom affectionately calling Dad, "You ole fart!"

Acknowledgments

I send a big hug and shout out to my sister-in-law, Mary Fehrenbacher Deters. Without her gentle encouragement, I never would have written these childhood memories.

I owe a big hug and an enormous bouquet of balloons to my partner, Worthy Durgin, who offered suggestions and steadfast encouragement not only on my writing journey but also on any path I explored.

Worthy Durgin left the Earth while this memoir was in the process of being published. My bouquet of balloons have floated up to him. I take comfort knowing Worthy is just a thought away.

Anita

Preface

"We didn't realize we were making memories. We just knew we were having fun." —Winnie The Pooh by A.A. Milne

"Never grow up. It's a trap." —Peter Pan by J. M. Barrie

I was a rambunctious little girl who loved riding my bike with the wind blowing through my hair. This rambunctiousness followed me into adolescence and adulthood. I had a passion for learning and adventure and often found myself in unusual situations. I never found life on the farm boring. With imagination and a fondness for escapades, I embraced the world around me and the simple pleasures of life at the end of a country lane.

This book holds the keys to a childhood rich with experience and wonder. I share many escapades and misadventures that bring laughter to my heart after all these years.

To my family and friends from the Green Creek area:

What I express on these pages are my memories and my perspective of what happened. If my stories of the past bring a few laughs and perhaps a few snorts and giggles about my skewed perspective of daily life on our farm, then I will be filled with joy. If my written memories cause you to feel upset in any way, I apologize. I also encourage you to write your recollections, as I would love to see Green Creek through your lenses.

—Anita Deters

Table of Contents

Dedication v

Acknowledgments vi

Preface viii

Chapter One
They Called Me Strawberry..1

Chapter Two
Bunny Adventures..12

Chapter Three
Terry the Eggman..17

Chapter Four
Flying Feathers in the Barnyard 24

Chapter Five
Dorothy...32

Chapter Six
Sticky Mess...38

Chapter Seven
Movie Musings..46

Chapter Eight
New Year's Eve..52

Chapter Nine
Confraternity...58

Chapter Ten
First Grade in Green Creek Elementary School.........62

Chapter 11
Mrs. Kirk and Bringing Down the House....................70

Chapter 12
Sr. Kathleen Throwing Down!...79

Chapter 13
Sister Barbara and Final Days of the Good Life.........86

Chapter 14
After 4:00 P.M..98

Chapter 15
Awk and Not..105

Chapter 16
Front Yard Follies...110

Chapter 17
December Delights 118

Chapter 18
Travels..121

Chapter 19
No Other Than My Mother..124

Chapter 20..126

About the Author...128

Chapter One
They Called Me Strawberry

I took my first breath on June 3, 1960, in a small farming community known as Green Creek. It is appropriate that I was born on a Friday since that was my favorite day of the week for most of my life. That day turned out to be a special one for my mom and dad because I was to be their last child of seven.

1960 was a bumper crop year for strawberries. When it came to planting and gardening and butchering, my mom did nothing in a small way. Thus, we had a huge strawberry patch planted next to our long, dusty lane. As the story goes, I was born while my eldest sister was on her senior high school graduation trip to Washington, D.C. When Mom decided to take a trip herself to the hospital to deliver me, she and Dad got in the black Chevy and drove past the strawberry patch. My mother yelled out the window to my siblings, who were picking strawberries, "Keep on picking! I am going to the hospital to have a baby!" As a result, except for my eldest sibling who was on the high school class trip, my siblings christened me "Strawberry" right then and there. Thank goodness the name did not stick.

After I was born, our neighbor Hilda came over with her own two-month-old baby girl, Gail, to help my siblings pick and prepare the strawberries for freezing while Mom recuperated from giving birth. After such a plentiful crop, our family was on strawberry overload. I don't know if this prompted an innate hatred of picking strawberries or that feeling grew after spending long unbearable hours hunched over in the hot June sun picking hundreds of quarts of those damn strawberries. The torture only began with the picking. I then had to stand for hours at the kitchen table washing and de-stemming them. My thumb would get a bruise on the end from days of de-stemming and would become tender, sore, and painful to the touch. This pain caused me to use a different finger, which proved to be awkward but at least wasn't painful. Oh, how I despised the entire strawberry picking and freezing process. One of my sisters declared she did not like strawberries; therefore, she did not have to pick. Liar, liar, pants on fire!! She never ate them at the dinner table, but I just knew she surely snuck a strawberry or two.

A GAL GROWING UP GREEN CREEK

The only good thing about strawberries was eating them. They were mouthwatering in the patch, but once my mother added a cup of sugar and poured the mixture on a piece of shortening cake, I could not resist! The sweet juice sank into the porous cake, creating a scrumptious dessert. She also made strawberry-rhubarb jam, which was equally tasty.

Was eating the desserts and jams worth the hard labor of picking and preparing strawberries? I am going to surprise you with a vehement, "Hell no!!" No dessert or jam could ever be worth the price of picking quart after quart of strawberries in the blistering heat of summer.

Many, many years later, after the trauma of picking strawberries had somewhat lessened in my memories, my significant other asked me to go strawberry picking with him. He envisioned it as a romantic experience we could enjoy together on a beautiful June afternoon. He obviously had watched too many Cary Grant movies.

No sooner had the invitation come out of his mouth than I became unglued. "What?! Are you kidding me?! Hell no! I am never, ever going to pick another strawberry in my life.

ANITA C. DETERS

I have had that lovely experience, and, no, I am not going strawberry picking. Did you hear that? The answer is 'No!'" We did not go strawberry picking.

Ten years went by after that initial invitation to pick strawberries. I had retired from being a schoolteacher, and I was enjoying a lovely June morning by chatting with my neighbor Jane.

Jane asked, "Hey, would you like to go with me to the strawberry field to pick a bit? It's such a beautiful day out. I think it would be a fun thing to do."

Well, my body tensed as I geared up for my response. But I seemed to sense a slight tap on my shoulder and a voice whispered, "Watch what you say and how you say it."

"Sure," I responded calmly. "It does seem like a perfect day to pick some strawberries."

I drove with my neighbor down to a local strawberry field. I paid for the quart container and hesitantly stepped my way onto the field. Lo and behold, the rows of strawberry plants were in raised beds! There was a reasonable two to three feet between each row. I assumed my picking position, being assured that I would not have strawberry stains all over my body and clothes when I finished my task.

The strawberries were bright red, juicy, and plentiful. No siblings complaining that I wasn't picking fast enough and throwing strawberries at me and no Mom telling me to quit eating and pick more and more! I heard only friendly chatter from two rows over. I looked up at the birds flying over and paused to listen to and try to interpret their calls.

I stopped picking and walked up and down the rows, marveling at the greens and the reds all mixed together. Above me, the sky glistened bright blue. Jane was correct. Indeed, it was a perfect day to pick strawberries.

Hilda and Gail

What a great friend and neighbor Hilda had been to help my mom with the freezing and preparing of strawberries after I was born, especially since little Gail was only two months old at the time. Years later, Hilda started a pinochle group of eight women that met once a month on Thursdays. My mom was in that group. The host of the pinochle group gave away three prizes, one for the highest total score, one for the lowest score (otherwise known as the booby prize), and one for the last woman to receive 100 aces in her hand. The pinochle group continued for decades. When a member of the group sadly passed away, another woman was asked to join.

Since the group started before Gail and I entered elementary school, we were the only kids hauled along with this fun group. Gail and I remain friends to this day. Gail and I spent many a good time jumping around in the hayloft of the barn without a care in the world. We typically played dodge ball or some other kid's game. However, Gail was a tad ornery, and she took an ink pen and scribbled all over my Barbie doll case. I was furious. I loved my Barbie dolls! I can laugh now when I think of the incident. I still remind Gail about it every once in a while.

After Mom passed at the age of 93, I wrote a poetic tribute to her on her birthday. These words express Mom's competitive style.

Happy Birthday!
Thinking of my mom today
You know she just always had to have her way!
"Move fast; don't go so slow.
What's wrong with you? Don't you know I want to go, go, go!!!
Do this.
Do that.
Go here. Go there.

Can you imagine Spirit telling Mom to go to her final rest?
"Oh, go away, you damn pest.
My Canasta cards aren't worn out yet!
And who will tell the great-grands
What this game is all about?"

If you knew G'ma, get out those cards tonight,
Pound your fist with delight
...and BEGIN
"Play hard, play fast,
But for God's sake
Play to WIN!

Miss you, Mom!

Blackberries

I don't remember which summer month was dedicated to blackberry picking, but I know it came after strawberry picking. I hated gathering blackberries, but at least it did not go on and on and on like the awful chore of harvesting strawberries. Again, Mom would make blackberry pies, blackberry cobbler, and blackberry jam. Oh, how delicious and mouthwatering they were, especially with a big scoop of ice cream on top. Pie a la mode—yum!! And there is nothing more soothing and yummier than a big scoop of jam, either strawberry or blackberry, on a large slice of freshly baked bread. I can smell that heavenly fragrance of freshly baked bread just by conjuring up the memory.

Blackberry season started when Dad or Mom entered the house, proclaiming they had found a trove of snarly, thorny bushes filled with juicy blackberries out in the woods. Oh, how I wished my parents would quit tromping in the woods and leave the exploring to us kids. But, no, they couldn't help themselves. They knew those blackberries were out there! Mom and Dad verbally directed the cows to lead them to a new patch every year. And just like us kids, those cows knew there would be hell to pay if they did not follow Mom and Pop's orders! So the cows inevitably led them to the wild blackberry bushes.

Soon we dug the tin gallon buckets out of hiding, and Mom searched the pantry for the glass jar of sulfur. We smeared the yellow powder all over our bodies and into crevices to prevent chiggers from biting us. I wondered if there was a scientific study to prove sulfur warded off chiggers. In my experience, it definitely does not. I always seemed to come home from picking blackberries with a mess of chigger bites. Torture. Those bites were absolute torture.

The evening before picking day, Mom warned us that we would have to wake up at 5:00 a.m. and hurry downstairs. The goal was to rise bright and early so we could finish picking blackberries before the heat and humidity of the day became unbearable and in hopes the chiggers, mosquitoes, and snakes would still be slumbering.

On the day of blackberry picking, I sleepily dragged myself out of bed and put on my oldest and the loosest fitting of my old, worn-out farm clothes. We sometimes went without underwear because chiggers like to burrow and bite around tight-fitting clothes. We dug our hands into the jar of sulfur and rubbed the yellow powder all around our body, paying close attention to the waistline, groin, and armpits. After grabbing a gallon tin bucket, we stepped groggily out the door, all headed for the woods. Mom and Dad stopped us once we got past the barnyard fence to receive our assignments, which included which direction to head towards.

"Some wild patches are up that hill and around the curve. You know, by the big oak tree."

"What oak tree?"

"You know. That big old oak tree."

Their directions were ridiculous. The woods were full of trees and a creek, small streams, hills, and valleys. We somehow found those wild patches and began picking before the sun and elementals became too *friendly*. The bushes were full of small, sharp thorns, and a picker was sure to get pricked multiple times.

Thankfully, our buckets didn't have to be full before we headed back to the house because some years the blackberry bushes were full of berries, and some years they were not. I think we all hated picking those berries, so Mom relaxed a bit about the quantity in the tin buckets.

Once we made it back home, we took off our clothes and waited our turn to take a bath to wash off the sulfur and bugs, spiders, and other creepy crawlies. This was a time when we made an exception to the rule of taking only our weekly Saturday evening bath. My one and only brother used to say, "We all take a bath on Saturdays whether we need it or not."

Once we had bathed and scrubbed the elements off of us, we gathered around the table and washed the blackberries in cold water in huge white ceramic pots. Mom would spend the rest of the morning baking blackberry pies and cobblers.

With a snap of the finger, I can actually smell the baking pie crusts and hear my mom's pleasant conversation as she danced and pranced around the kitchen in her worn housedress and apron, bare feet, doing what she did best. How much better can life be with a happy mom and tired kids?

Chapter Two
Bunny Adventures

Spring always brings to mind a memory of a silly tradition my family had. My mom brought this unusual annual event into my family. Her family had done the same during her upbringing in rural Illinois in an area known as Island Grove. Now, you will not find Island Grove on a map. Local folks from this part of the state just know where Island Grove is, just as they do Green Creek, where I spent my childhood. We actually pronounce it Green Crick.

The day before Easter, Holy Saturday as it is called by some, my siblings and I would call in the Easter Bunny. We were convinced the Easter Bunny would lay no eggs for us on Sunday if we did not invite him on Saturday. This was a big production. Reflecting on it, I think the "calling in" had more to do with Mom wanting us all out of the house for a good part of the day.

A GAL GROWING UP GREEN CREEK

First, we had to mow at least a small portion of our huge, slightly hilly lawn. We had to do sufficient mowing to make enough grass clippings for several bunny nests. Some years, my sister closest to me in age, Evelyn, and I would start gathering flowers and twigs and whatever we felt would please the bunny. These flowers and twigs would go into his nest a week before the big calling-in ceremony. I don't know why, but I always think of the Easter Bunny of the male persuasion, even though he lays eggs.

After making nests, we kids planned what time the ceremony would take place and then promptly headed on out to the chicken house at the appointed hour. Now, this was not a chicken house with one, two, or even twenty birds. No, we were chicken farmers; at least my mom was. Mom raised hens. Dad had cows.

My siblings and I went into the nastiest smelling chicken house with hundreds of hens in it. If we were lucky, the old hens were out, and only the new pullets or even little peeps were in the chicken house. Little chicks were fun. Old hens were just plain nasty and stinky. We joyfully entered this shed, gathered in a circle, and sang our welcoming song to the Easter

ANITA C. DETERS

Bunny with a choir of hens in the background clucking harmony. The oldest sister available led the event. We would sing, "Here Comes Peter Cottontail." After the song, we would go around the circle and call out what we wanted the bunny to bring to us.

"Louder!" the lead sister would shout. "Do you really think the bunny can hear you? Louder, I say. Louder!!"

I will say she must have been on a bit of a power kick during this ceremony. She must have felt quite empowered since mom was back in the house and now this sister could wear the crown of leadership.

"Black jelly beans!"

"Chocolate eggs! Bird eggs!"

We called out a large assortment of candies, as we each had a different favorite. At the end of our proclamation, the leader decided we needed to give the bunny more time to lay our treats, so again we traveled in a small circle, singing "Here Comes Peter Cottontail" in that nasty smelling hen house.

"OK! That should be enough time for the bunny to do his duty!" the leader would announce, and off we went to where we made our bunny nests to see if the bunny had laid what we asked for. We were always surprised and delighted to find the bunny had placed our choices in the nests with obvious care. I could never figure out how such big feet could lay the candy in such a carefully assembled arrangement. We only chose the greenest and fluffiest grass we could find, and the bunny sure appreciated that extra effort! We were delighted that the calling-in ceremony went as planned, and we were sure to get hundreds of colored eggs on Easter Sunday morning!!

It wasn't until I had a teaching position in Jasper County, Illinois, that I found a co-worker who also had this tradition in her family. Now, Jasper County was in the woods and the people were kind and friendly—good country folk. My dad called them River Rats because the Embarras River ran through the county. Teaching positions in Jasper County were coveted because teachers there were paid very well thanks to the power plant. This co-worker grew up in a little area called Valentine. Nobody had ever heard of Valentine, and it definitely was not on the map so far as I know. It was quite close to Island Grove, where my mother grew up, so that is likely how the calling-in ceremony had the bunny hopping from Valentine to Island Grove and finally to Green Creek. I still treasure the memory of that quirky yet sacred ceremony. It remains one of my favorite memories. I must admit to being a little disappointed that my siblings chose not to carry on this tradition with their families.

Easter always sends me back in time and has me singing "Here Comes Peter Cottontail" while chewing black jelly beans, which was what I always shouted for the Easter Bunny to bring me! To this day, I can't resist building a grass nest in the yard on Holy Saturday with a giant grin on my face.

Chapter Three
Terry the Eggman

One of the most hilarious memories I have involves a favorite character of mine, Terry the Eggman, as we referred to him. Terry frequently dropped by our century-old white farmhouse when I was growing up. This gentleman resembled Howard Sprague from *The Andy Griffith Show*, perhaps a bit taller with longer legs and a little more gray in his hair. He sported the same type of boxy mustache as Howard Sprague.

I don't know how Mom came in contact with Terry the Eggman but he played a significant role in the egg business she managed. During the 1960s and 70s, the egg business was lucrative. Years after her egg business was no more than a distant memory, Mom pulled out her ledger to prove that to one of my nephews when he inquired about it.

ANITA C. DETERS

    Terry the Eggman was a bus driver. His route took him from Effingham, Illinois, to Chicago on a regular basis, a 200-mile trek. Like many of us, Terry had a side hustle, which was selling eggs to restaurants in Chicago. Sometimes, Terry would travel down the country roads and turn into our quarter mile dusty, bumpy lane and pick up three or four cases of eggs. Those who did not grow up gathering eggs, washing them in the machine, scrubbing them with a brush to make them extra clean, kenneling the eggs, and rubbing them with sandpaper to make them shine may not be aware that a case of eggs holds 30 dozen, and those cases were quite heavy! My mom or one of us kids or Terry would haul those cases of eggs up from the damp and musty cellar to Terry's bus or truck, depending on what he drove that day. When Terry drove the Greyhound bus, he would put the eggs in the compartment that held the luggage.

    Now, we all liked Terry. He was a personable guy, not a smart aleck, just a nice man who liked us kids and respected Mom and Dad. He was great to do business with. He sometimes requested that Mom sell him old eggs because the cooks at the restaurants said they splattered out bigger in the skillet. Who knew? Also, when we were kenneling and saw that there were two yolks in the egg, Mom would be sure Terry would get that egg because the cooks really liked the double yolk eggs. City folks are so crazy!

Mom's only complaint about Terry was that he always arrived at the same time Walter Cronkite was on TV. Terry would make himself comfortable in front of the TV, spread out those long legs, and settle in to watch the news. We all had to walk around those long legs. "And that's the way it is" was Terry's signal to get up and stretch and say goodbye. Terry the Eggman was just another regular fixture in our living area. Dad would be out in the milkhouse when Terry visited, but Mom still had to contend with some man stretching out in the middle of the room and having to walk around or over those long legs.

During one of Terry's visits, Mom was still down in the cellar kenneling eggs, perhaps preparing the last case of eggs for pick up. Terry settled in his chair only for a few minutes and then got up to go to the bathroom. That was when the unthinkable happened. Terry walked into that bathroom and closed that bathroom door—hard!

All our neighbors, friends, and relatives had been around enough to know that one never, ever closed our bathroom door because it would not open. Did I mention I grew up in a century-old farmhouse? It creaked and groaned constantly. Why bother shutting the front door? Wind blew through it like it was open anyway. Nothing about the foundation was carpenter square. And the bathroom door—well, let me tell you, that door no longer fit in the doorway, especially during the summer when it was humid! That old wooden door would swell up, and nobody was going to convince it to shut. Nobody!! Except Terry. He did the unthinkable.

An important part of the outrageousness of this story was the size of our bathroom. It was not more than five feet square. You could barely turn around in it. It had room for a single sink to the left, a bathtub two feet straight ahead, and a toilet on the right *behind* that swollen door that swung inward instead of out into the hall. If you were washing your hands at the sink, you could not see the person sitting on the toilet because the door hid them. When you opened the door, it just barely missed the edge of the sink.

When Terry shut the bathroom door hard, my older sister, Evelyn, and I looked at each in horror and disbelief.

"Go tell Mom," Evelyn commanded.

Now, I usually did what my elders told me without much of a fuss, because most things just didn't matter that much to me, but I wasn't stupid! My mom was a forceful storm to be reckoned with.

"Oh, no, you go tell her!" I quickly retorted.

"No! You tell her!"

Well, after several exchanges, Evelyn came to the realization there was no way in hell I was going to tell Mom about the crisis in the bathroom. Evelyn ventured down into the deep musty abyss, the cellar, where Mom was working hurriedly to pack up the last case of eggs. I waited upstairs for the reaction. I knew it wasn't going to be pretty.

"Oh, *shit*!"

I am quite sure Terry the Eggman heard Mom's thundering response as well.

Mom and Evelyn came running up the steps from the cellar. Terry was already vehemently shaking and rattling that poor old door. Mom was beside herself. Dad was milking cows, so this was all on her. Terry shook the door so hard I thought the house would come down.

"Terry, stop! Just stop shaking the door! It ain't going to open! Try to open the window."

Thank goodness the window high above the tub was known to open. Well, probably it was never known to be shut.

"Terry, you are going to have to crawl through the window," Mom said emphatically.

"What?!" Terry's reaction was almost as vehement as Mom's.

While Terry was in the bathroom pondering how he would manipulate and contort his body through the window located five feet up above the bathtub, Mom went across the barnyard into a shed and got a ladder. The ladder would help Terry's descent from the window and would allow him to avoid the big, old bushy bush outside under that window.

I don't know how Terry maneuvered that long-legged body of his, but I suppose where there is a will there is a way. It took a lot of encouragement from my sister, Mom and me, but eventually he made it out of the window. We watched from the outside as Terry accomplished this feat. First one leg, then an arm, then his torso, and then the other side of his body made it out of the bathroom window into the outside world. He carefully placed his foot on a ladder rung and started his descent.

I don't remember if we all started laughing when Terry escaped from the bathroom. I seriously doubt it, but that memory sure has brought some huge belly laughs in the years since.

I do not recall how the bathroom door finally opened. I think somebody had to climb the ladder again and entered through the window to work on the door. I know for sure the door was not removed from the hinges. We may have used the outhouse until the humidity went down and the bathroom door opened again. All I know for sure is the bathroom door did eventually open. And I also recall for sure that nobody, nobody ever shut that door again.

Chapter Four
Flying Feathers in the Barnyard

Many footprints were embedded in our barnyard. The cows took a leisurely stroll twice daily to and from the barn with their heads bobbing and their bags slowly swinging like a metronome to their gait. The cows always looked so calm, knowing they would soon be relieved of their heavy bags of milk. Just like those cows, I found the daily walk from the farmhouse to the milking parlor to do chores to be a relaxing, soothing, and somehow a satisfying stroll. I loved this part of my day. I also loved butchering day in the barnyard!

Imagine a huge barnyard that had a dirt path big enough for a milk truck to drive up to the white stone milk parlor. A small creek also ran through this barnyard. There was a milking parlor, a hay barn with a loft, a huge red machine shed, and an old, dilapidated shed about to fall down that housed a 54 Chevy. This shed housed a bin where we kept the chicken feed. I loved the smell of those big gray pellets of chicken feed. This bin held a truck load or maybe two loads of them. Behind the shed and to the side were the fenced in chicken yard and chicken house where hundreds of chickens enjoyed their grand life until that fateful day when Mom would call out early in the morning, "Today is butchering day!"

My mom didn't do anything in a small way. No, sir. Butchering day meant no fewer than and probably way more than 100 chickens would be slaughtered and put into our freezer by 5:00 p.m. The process had to be completed by that time because the cows would saunter on up to the barnyard, waiting to be milked then. Those bossies looked forward to the steady pump of the milking machine to offer relief from their full bags. Also, butchering day had to occur after the state milk inspector had made his annual visit. I don't think the milking parlor would have passed state inspection if the inspector spotted all those feathers and chicken innards anywhere near the bulk tank of raw milk.

Reflecting back on it, butchering day must have been a major undertaking for Mom and Dad. They planned for weeks in advance because

ANITA C. DETERS

Mom had to freeze gallons of water in plastic milk jugs that she borrowed from friends and relatives that bought milk at the store. A couple of my older sisters were married by this time, and they too would freeze water in gallon milk jugs. In addition to collecting plastic jugs, they needed at least one hundred milk cartons because, once the hen was butchered, the legs, thighs, wings, breast, and neck along with gizzards, livers, and hearts were placed in these milk cartons and then frozen. Mom instructed us in how to put each part of the chicken in a carton, just like puzzle pieces. We packed each carton the same way. If we did it correctly, the eight pieces of chicken fit perfectly in the quart milk carton. Mom was a smart woman, and because of her strategizing, butchering day ran smoothly and quickly. If not, we all had hell to pay.

    The big hunks of ice were placed in the water tanks where the butchered hens would be thrown as their bodies were cut apart. This operation was run like a Ford factory assembly line. Now, I am not saying it was the most sanitary of operations, but I suppose it really was not any more unsanitary than what goes on in any food plant. Anyhow, everybody had their job assignment given to them early in the morning. There was a hierarchy of tasks. If you proved you were good at one job, you would gradually be promoted to the next duty either that day or the following year.

Chicken hooks were handed out to the kids, which included me. My nieces and nephews who were close to my age received a hook too. We ran around that chicken yard and hooked the chicken's legs and delivered the captured hen to my mom. We had so much fun chasing those squawking chickens around the chicken house yard. And, honestly, my mom loved watching us, and she had fun too as she gleefully waited on a stump with a wooden block between her legs and a hatchet in hand. We ran up to mom with our catch and took the chicken off the hook, handed the hen to Mom where she would give the hen one final massage under her arm, smooth down the feathers, and lay that poor unsuspecting chicken on the block. With a powerful blow, off went the chicken's head. Mom would throw the headless chicken to the side. We were mesmerized as we watched that headless hen jump around like it was a kernel of popcorn in hot oil. After a while, we transported these dead hens by hand or wheelbarrow to the barnyard where the next step occurred.

As this was going on, Dad heated the water in five-gallon buckets. The water had to be boiling hot so the feathers could be plucked easily. Dad or some other elder would hold them by the feet and dunk the headless hens in the water three or four times and then take each one out and swing it around a few times so the hot water would fly off the hen. Then he handed off the body to a kid to remove the feathers. It was quite a mess. This job wasn't all that easy because the hen really had to be plucked clean. Sometimes we would have to give the old hen a second dunk into the hot water to loosen the feathers. The barnyard eventually would be covered with white chicken feathers. It was a circus. After the hen was naked of feathers, it was brought into the milk house and placed into the icy water where the butchering and packing took place.

My sister Evelyn and my brother, George, took great pride in pulling out the craw of the hens. They then blew into the craw, thinking they could crow like a chicken. I thought it was so gross to pull out the inside of a chicken and then blow into a piece of it just so you could sound like a crowing hen. On the other hand, I loved cleaning out the gizzard, especially when there was a bunch of chicken feed in it. The gizzard had a tough lining which I thought was fun to pull apart and clean.

One year, my brother created an electric chicken plucker. This piece of equipment was quite ingenious. He collected 30 or 40 old milk insulators, which were rubber liners that protected the cow's udders as they were being milked and were the shape of a long udder, if you can envision that. Then somehow he attached the insulators, five in a row with rows one or two inches apart, around a small wheel or some cylinder object. The insulators looked like the spokes on a wheel, except there was no rim on this wheel, just the insulators. This object with the milk insulators was put on a motorized rotary and placed above a deep sink. When used, the feathers would fall into this outdoor sink. Using an extension cord from the shed to the barnyard, my brother plugged in the machine, and those insulators went round and round and round, whirled and whirled like an airplane propeller at an uncontrollable speed. It was hilarious. We laughed so hard at that contraption. My dad stood off to the side and grinned his huge, toothy grin. I think he was rather proud of the ingenuity of his son. He enjoyed our laughter and got a few chuckles out of it too. The chickens not so much.

The person who performed the plucking job would take a hot, wet, headless hen with feathers and hold it over the wheel with the insulators on it while this electric plucker basically beat off the feathers. What a riot! The trick was not to put too much pressure on the hen as you held it on the wheel. If you did, the hen ended up being a glob of goo flesh in your hands. But, once you got the knack of the correct pressure to hold onto the hen, the feathers came off quite nicely, and all you had to do was a little finishing up work and pluck the smallest of the feathers. Of course, the hen would be a tad bit bruised, but, hey, we weren't selling these butchered birds. We were just eating them.

Somewhere in the course of this early morning, Mom would sneak away and prepare the noon meal. What do you think we had for our noon meal? If you guessed fried chicken, you are correct. Nobody complained because we just weren't allowed to complain in my family, but several people passed on that platter of fried chicken. It is difficult to swallow fried chicken when the smell of raw chicken is on your hands. I have a sister who is in her seventies, and to this day she still will not eat chicken because she says she just can't get that smell of raw chicken off her hands.

This major operation was completed by 5 p.m. We fought over who got the heart to eat when chicken was our meal. All went into the freezer. The following day, we cleaned the barnyard, burning the chicken feathers in the burn barrel and giving the milking parlor a good scrubbing and sanitizing.

I wish somebody had taken pictures of the barnyard covered with feathers, of that crazy electric chicken plucking machine that George made, and of 10 or more kids running around hooking hens by their legs. I wish I had a photo of Mom's joy as she brought down the hatchet, but nobody thought to mark the occasion. To us, it was just another crazy day in the life of our Midwestern farm family.

Chapter Five
Dorothy

My mom's sister lived about three miles down the road from us. Both sisters had married and moved from Island Grove to Green Creek, all of about 40 miles away. Mom met Dad at a barn dance. He was 10 years older. She was 16. She told me once that Grandma had no idea that Dad was 10 years older, and she threatened me not to tell her mother. Now, I remember, Mom said this to me with a grin, so I am not sure if she was pulling my leg or not. This was my mom's nature. One always had to wonder about her stories.

Mom and her sister, well, actually, her half-sister, talked daily on the phone. Mom was six years older than Dorothy, and I think in many ways Mom still felt responsible for her. Mom was the oldest in her family, and she always said her stepfather made her take care of all of her half brothers and sisters. He was not kind to her.

A GAL GROWING UP GREEN CREEK

Dorothy was born premature. When she was an infant, Grandma would open the door to the oven, place Dorothy in a shoebox, and then put the shoebox with Dorothy inside on the oven door during the day. At night, Grandma opened a bureau drawer and Dorothy slept inside it. Dorothy never grew to be big, maybe five feet tall—if that.

In spite of being small in stature, Dorothy gave birth to 13 healthy children. These kids were smart! Their professions included doctor, optometrist, teacher, nurse, accountant, computer technician, and butcher.

Did you hear me say 13 children? Where I hail from, huge families were not uncommon. I was raised in a German Catholic farming community, and kids 10 years and up were driving tractors around the countryside and pulling huge wagons of hay bales, and nobody thought a thing of it. The teachers in my four-room country schoolhouse were aghast at the numbers of siblings we all had. One day, a teacher went around the room asking, "How many kids are in your family?" She got answers of 9, 8, 10, 13—the number went as high as 16. I remember slumping down farther and farther in my seat. When the teacher asked me, I said softly, "seven." I was so embarrassed. What the hell was wrong with my parents?! Why didn't they have more kids?!

Well, the saying on Facebook is that your first best friends are your cousins. That certainly was the case for me. I loved going over to Dorothy's house and playing with my cousins. Dorothy would greet Mom and me on the front porch with one baby suckling from her breast and another hanging on her leg. Always. Always a baby suckling and a baby hanging on her leg. Dorothy constantly had a twinkle in her eye. She talked so fast to my mom that a pool of spit would collect on the right corner of her mouth, and that spit never had a chance to drop or slobber down her chin. It just hung there. I was engrossed by her fast flying tongue and remember staring up at Dorothy, wondering when all that spit would drop. It never did. I don't think I ever really listened to anything Dorothy said, because I was always daydreaming about how this short woman walked around all day long with one baby hanging from her boob and another clutching her leg with her tongue flying. How did this little woman keep it all together?

Now, Dorothy drove a huge station wagon. When she went to town, barreling down the country roads, the kids' heads and arms would be flying, waving, and bouncing out the windows. Mom said Dorothy drove like a bat out of hell. When Dorothy flew by, it looked like the car was driving itself. She was so small you couldn't see her head over the steering wheel. Mom said sometimes Dorothy would put catalogs and phone books on her seat so she could see over the steering wheel, but the problem was then she couldn't reach the pedal. It was comical yet scary. Dorothy also didn't have the best eyesight. If my memory serves me correctly, she had several surgeries on her eyes, but this did not deter her from driving into town and all over the countryside.

Train tracks in my area ran parallel to Highway 45. This meant one had to go over the tracks on the way into town and to cross them several times to get to the grocery stores once in town. Now, for our protection, these tracks had automated crossing arms that came down when a train was coming. However, sometimes they would go down and stay in that position for hours, so this safeguard wasn't too reliable. Unless you wanted to sit at the crossing all day, staring at those arms with no train coming, you would drive around these arms.

I think you may already have a sneaking suspicion of where this story is going. That is correct. Not once but twice, Dorothy was unsuccessful in her attempt to drive around these arms. She misjudged the distance, or maybe she just couldn't see. She knocked out the entire front windshield of the station wagon. Twice. I can only imagine what her husband, Lawrence, had to say. There was only one person I know that cussed more than my mom, and that was Lawrence. I don't believe they made any babies those nights after Dorothy hit the crossing arms.

After knocking out two windshields, I think Mom actually became quite frightened of Dorothy's driving abilities. If we kids were going somewhere on our bicycles, Mom would say, "Now, if you see Dorothy coming, be sure to get off your bikes and go into the ditch."

And when we were in our car and Mom was a passenger, she would get panicky and yell, "Here comes Dorothy! Move over! Quick! I said move over!!"

These two sisters, friends, and neighbors both lived well into their 90s. My heart filled with compassion for Dorothy at Mom's wake. How difficult it must be to lose a best friend and sister at the same time. At the service, Dorothy still had a twinkle in her eye, but her tongue did not fly nearly as fast, and her thoughts seemed a bit confused. Having 13 kids will do that to you, I suppose. She said goodbye to Mom with a smile on her face. Together, they experienced the best life has to offer, a good friend to share daily stories and big laughs about broken windshields.

Chapter Six
Sticky Mess

I have always enjoyed riding a bicycle. Even as a little girl, nothing gave me more pleasure than hopping on an old beat-up bike and racing down our dusty lane filled with holes and bumps and crevices. I would turn a sharp right by the huge old oak tree which marked the end of our dusty lane. Once I was on the paved country road, I would ride my bike, swerving to the left and then to the right, and sometimes I pedaled smoothly with no hands on the handlebars. Plastic tassels that I ordered from the back of a cereal box adorned my handlebars. I felt free with the wind blowing through my hair and the hot sun beating down on me. I loved every minute of my summer! I would bike down to the corner stop sign and then turn around and go back home. It was just enough of a break from Mom's constant barrage of orders around the house to get me singing again. I took those short bike rides several times a day. In the late afternoon, just before dusk, I would sneak away on my bike and ride around the country block, which was three to five miles long, depending on the route I chose to take.

My parents must have known how happy I was on a bike because I asked for a new Schwinn bicycle and got one with no hesitation from Mom or Dad. I remember going into town with Dad and visiting the bicycle shop where a hundred or more Schwinn bicycles were on display. I picked out a green one and rode that bike the seven miles back to our house in the country. Those were the days!

Those fantastic bike riding days were only interrupted by one event: the oiling of the roads by the county maintenance crew. We all dreaded that time of the summer. They spread a thick layer of gooey tar on the roads, and after this hot tar cooled a bit, they added a thick layer of chat. Chat is comprised of pebbles that are layered on top of the oil. Chat is an important part of this process because these country roads had to endure months of snow and ice. First, the crew oiled one side of the road and then the other. Farm wives going into town to get groceries during this time chose which side of the road would be less of a mess on the vehicle, because oil and chat would fly onto wheels, fenders, and every place else. I can still hear the deafening ping, ping, ping as it flew up onto the car, and I knew I would have to clean all that off the car fenders and doors. It was a sticky and messy job.

Even though we lived down a long lane, we could smell the hot tar permeating the air. The odor of petroleum was a sure indication the maintenance crew was doing their thing, and soon I would be doing my thing of cleaning oil and tar off the car.

For a bike rider, the oiled roads presented a real problem. Even if I stayed way to the side of the road, the tar always managed to aggravate me. Sometimes I ended up with a big gooey ball inside the fender of the bike. I would have no choice but to stop and dig it out because this ball of black tar would stop the mechanics of the bike. The pedals simply would not budge.

One hot summer day when the roads were being oiled, my sister and I were invited to a campout by one of our girlfriends who lived several miles down from our own country home. The campout was going to start in the midafternoon so we could play ball and other games into the evening. It was bound to be a great time!

My sister and I left that afternoon on our bikes, carrying homemade cookies with us that we would share with our friends. The roads were heavily oiled with thick tar, but the chat was not yet on the road. Even though we rode our bikes near the ditch where tall weeds grew, some of that oil started to collect on the rims of our bikes. There was a cornfield on the right side of us. It must have been July because the corn was five feet tall or more and looked like a wall of green. On the left side of the road, a beautiful alfalfa field shone in the intense sunlight. Waves of heat hovered above the fields.

In my mind, it was a perfect afternoon—until the most God awful event of my life occurred. As my sister and I approached the corner where the stop sign was staked, we stopped and assessed the situation. We had no choice but to cross over the newly tarred road.

My sister looked at me and said, "You go."

I looked at her. *Why me? Why do I have to go first*, I wondered.

"Go," she said in an authoritative voice.

After hesitating for a few seconds, I pushed off on my bike with a package of cookies under my arm, hoping for the best. My tires made several revolutions, and I was in the middle of the intersection where I pumped a bit harder.

Big mistake. The wheels slipped on the oil, and I went down in the middle of the intersection. One whole side of one leg and one arm were now covered in tar. I was stunned.

"Get up!" said my sister.

Without a word, I tried to position myself to get the bike off of me. I got half way up, and I slipped on the oil, and down I went again.

"Get up!" my sister yelled.

Once again, I tried, and down I went—again. The harder I tried to get up, the slipperier my shoes became, and the harder I fell into that gooey mess of black tar.

"Help me!" I yelled at my sister.

"Are you kidding me? I am not getting in that tar! Crawl out!"

Miraculously, I crawled out of that black, hot, sticky mess. My bike and the cookies stayed behind in the middle of the intersection.

Needless to say, I was covered from head to toe in black tar. My sister took her bike and followed behind me as we walked back home. I felt humiliated, frustrated, upset, and, needless to say, sticky. We walked down a row in the cornfield so no driver on the road could see me and my sister. Trekking through the cornfield provided some relief from the hot sun and the hot tar on my skin. It was a long, hot, depressing hike through the cornfields and along our dusty lane with the sun beating down on us. I felt absolutely miserable.

I walked into the front yard and then went around back where I knew Mom would be putzing around. Her mouth dropped when she saw me.

"What in the world?! How am I going to get all that tar off of you?"

I stood still and speechless, waiting for Mom's next action.

Mom's first step was to tell me to strip off my clothes. She stuffed them and my shoes in a paper sack that eventually ended up in the burn barrel. She then pulled a big washtub out of the small washhouse, which was a few steps away from the back porch. She ran back and forth from the gas tank in the barnyard with a five-gallon bucket filled with gasoline. I watched silently and stood naked in the backyard as she filled the washtub with gasoline. Mom then had me climb in and soak in the gasoline so the tar could start to dissolve. I did not cry. I did not scream. I did what I was told to do and sat down slowly in the tub filled with gasoline; however, I did plead.

"Please, Mom, please! Please! Please do not let Terry the Eggman come back here!!

Now, the fact that I was naked and could possibly be seen by Terry the Eggman did bother me. My bigger concern was that Terry the Eggman always, always had a cigar in his mouth. I was petrified that I would go up in flames if Terry the Eggman came moseying around to the backyard. I had a clear vision of me screaming in pain as I burnt to a crisp.

Mom assured me that Terry the Eggman would not come around to the back of the house. As I miserably soaked in that tub of gasoline, my mind was busy conjuring up a plan in case he did. I stayed alert to detect any noise or sighting of Terry the Eggman.

It seemed like I soaked forever in that tub. I wondered if the gas would somehow enter my innards and I would be damaged for life. With those fumes and chemicals, who knew what the consequences might be? Still, no sightings of Terry, the Eggman.

After a long soak in the gasoline and a hard scrubbing, I was taken to the bathroom where I soaked in a bathtub filled with cold water. I felt sure no amount of bathing would evaporate the fumes of gasoline off my body. I was a stinky mess into the evening.

Well, I did indeed survive that hot, horrid summer day. Life did go on. And somehow I still had a bicycle. I have no idea who retrieved it from the corner, what happened to the cookies, or what became of my sister after I entered the front yard of our old farmhouse.

I guess the fumes of the gasoline deleted some of my memories of that terrible day. However, I do remember one significant fact. Terry the Eggman did not show himself in the backyard on that horrific day. In spite of all the terrible feelings this day brought, I was and will always be thankful he did not saunter into the backyard on that scorching, eventful, exhausting summer day. Because of this, I was not burnt to a crisp, and I continued to enjoy riding my bike for many, many more years.

Chapter Seven
Movie Musings

The first movie I ever saw on the big screen was *Mary Poppins*, which was released in 1964 and starred Julie Andrews and Dick Van Dyke. I remember being so excited watching it at our local movie theatre, which was called The Heart, in downtown Effingham, Illinois.

I loved every bit of that Walt Disney musical production. I have no recollection of who went with me, but it must have been my mom because I remember shortly after attending that movie, Mom bought the musical album of *Mary Poppins*. I played that record over and over, singing and dancing in the living room all by myself, reliving the entire musical over and over.

The Sound of Music and *The Happiest Millionaire* both came out in 1967, and I enjoyed viewing them on the big screen at The Heart.

Once again, my mom bought the albums that accompanied these movies. What a treat!

Those three musical albums brought me many happy hours. I imagined myself on Broadway, and eruptions of applause filled my heart and my imagination!

Going to the movies was not a regular occurrence for me. It was a really special treat. One summer afternoon, my mom dropped me and two of my cousins, Cindy and Marilyn, my best friends at the time, off at the movie theatre. We were just little girls then. She left us without any supervision and trusted us to behave. We did not. We ran like wild stallions onto the second floor where the restrooms were located. The floor was covered in a soft, maroon paisley carpet. We played tag there for a short while until the manager came up and scolded us and told us to settle down. Of course, we replied with absolute fits of giggles and scurried downstairs. What was the movie? I have no idea, but it sure was a fun afternoon!

Going to the drive-in theatre was another whole adventure. Preparing for a trip to the drive-in was an undertaking all of its own. First, we popped the popcorn at home, filling several paper grocery bags to take with us and enjoy during the movie. Then, once we were there, we had to find the perfect parking spot to view the screen. Last but not least, it took some doing to configure the speakers and hook them to the rolled-down car window. The first movie I saw at the drive-in was *Old Yeller*. The car was packed with Dad, Mom, my brother, at least one other sister, and me. I remember my brother, George, giving me advice about what to do if I became scared during the movie.

"Anita, if you get scared, just stare up at those blinking red lights on the tower. That's what I do," he said, sharing his worldly piece of advice for me. Indeed, I had to take his advice, as that movie became quite frightening.

Once settled and before the movie began at the drive-in, our parents encouraged us to jump out of the car and run in front of the mighty outdoor screen where there were swings and slides for kids to play. I did so a little hesitantly. I think it was a strange environment for me, and I really did not want to lose sight of the car. I usually ran hurriedly back to the car after a few minutes, probably much to Mom and Dad's disappointment.

A few years later, when my cousins from Chicago came to town, one of my older sisters took them and me to the drive-in. We watched the first movie, and I remember my sister went through some mental turmoil, wondering if we should stay for the second movie, which was *Ben Hur*. She thought it would be too late and too graphic for us youngsters to watch. The decision was made to stay. I loved, loved, loved that movie. *Ben Hur* was so much better than the first movie we watched, which I don't even recall.

So began the daily ritual of going to the section of the daily newspaper and looking for movies that I might enjoy. When I spotted that *Ma and Pa Kettle* would be showing at the drive-in, I knew we would soon be popping bags of popcorn and loading up the car. My mom absolutely loved Ma and Pa Kettle! It was a comedy series that came out in the late 1940s and into the 1950s written about a hillbilly family with 15 kids with the last name of Kettle. Usually, Mom would ring up one of her girlfriends from across the field, and with mischievous delight she would excitedly yell into the telephone, "Hey, Verena! Ma and Pa Kettle are playing at the drive-in! Wanna go?"

I think Mom thought it was always necessary to yell into the phone because the person on the other end was miles away. Verena was a farm wife and never had children but she enjoyed being around them. She and Mom had the same salty sense of humor, and it was comical to watch them in action.

Mom, Verena, probably my sister, and I made the trip to the drive-in, and, of course, all of that popcorn went with us and was eaten. I loved Ma and Pa Kettle too, but even more I loved watching my mom explode with her huge belly laughs when she got tickled about an escapade happening on the giant screen in front of us. I was always laughing inside of myself, because I thought it interesting that, from my point of view, Mom was really watching her own life in front of her. Mom had a similar disposition to Ma Kettle, and Dad certainly reminded me of Pa Kettle, and the 15 children, well, while I didn't have 14 siblings, I sure had plenty of nieces, nephews, and cousins running around the house. I got such a kick out of Mom bursting with laughter about her own lifestyle.

As a teenager, my most profound memory at the drive-in was watching *Pinocchio: Something Grows But Not His Nose*. On a hot, humid summer evening, a bunch of us guys and gals gathered at the local graveled parking lot. We loaded up two pickup trucks with coolers of beer, lawn chairs, and ourselves. Some of us lay down on the bed of the truck and others didn't even bother trying to hide as we drove into the entrance of the drive-in. Once inside, the two trucks were backed into the parking spot side by side so we had opportune viewing, and we settled in for a good ole time. And boy was it ever!! We laughed and howled, drank beer, and hooted some more. This ridiculous soft porn movie was a riot to us! By the end of the movie, Pinocchio's private appendage had grown so long that he was walking behind a hay wagon with his appendage laid out across it. To us farm kids, we could relate to that hay wagon, and using it for this purpose was just too much! It was fun to be so silly, goofy, and, yes, probably a lot drunk.

I still enjoy a good comedy at the movies, but nothing will ever match that elated feeling of singing and dancing to Walt Disney productions, laughing at my own life review in the form of Ma and Pa Kettle, and being blissfully happy as an adolescent before the realization that there was more to life than growing appendages.

Chapter Eight
New Year's Eve

Every New Year's Eve, Mom and Dad celebrated with six or maybe eight other couples in the neighborhood. They rotated the houses where the celebration would occur. It was always a wild night for the kids too. New Year's Eve was crazy for both adults and kids. The excitement started building as soon as the women began to organize this annual whoop-de-do! They would get on the phone and try to remember who hosted the party the previous year and then would wait for somebody to volunteer to hold it this time. Once that was decided, the women started preparing snacks, sandwiches, and drinks they would bring to the hosts' home.

The adults spent the night playing Pinochle and drinking. When midnight struck, everyone blew noisemakers, popped balloons, and carried on loudly. Usually the kids started to drift off to sleep soon after the New Year was ushered in.

One year when my mom and dad hosted the party, after everybody cleared out, way past midnight, we smelled something burning. We searched everywhere. The smell could not be denied. Something was on fire. Finally, my sister Evelyn detected the problem. A balloon had landed on a light bulb and it was slowly melting. What a relief. A great way to ring in the new year knowing the house would not burn to the ground!

Now, here is the crazy part of this annual gathering. As years went on, the adults enjoyed the New Year's party more and more, and the house really started to rock 'n' roll with all sorts of ruckus and noise with all those people. So the moms decided it would be easier if the kids went to a separate house to party. It took some planning and thinking to figure out which house the kids would have and which house the adults would have for New Year's Eve. Yes, that is correct. The adults celebrated at one house, and the kids partied at another. They made an occasional phone call just to make sure all was well in the kids' house.

As time went on and the kids grew, the moms eventually decided that maybe the boys and girls needed to be separated for this annual party. So they put their heads together and chose which house would host the girls, which house would host the boys, and which house would host the adults. I loved these New Year's Eve parties! They were always so much fun!

It only took a year or two before the moms thought, "You know, it would really be great if we could unload these toddlers and babies on somebody." So the plan was that one year the house with the boys took care of the babies and toddlers, and the girls babysat them the next year. The arrangements almost took a ledger to organize the logistics of who was going where on which year. What a wild idea! But the uncanny thing is that it worked!

I asked Mom years later what in the world the adults were thinking to come up with letting kids party in their own house on New Year's Eve!! Mom just grinned and shook her head. She got this faraway look in her eyes like she was reliving those parties, and she softly giggled and said, "I don't know, Anita. I just don't know!"

Now, my dad passed at the age of 95. He was at least 10 to 20 years older than all those neighborly friends with whom he celebrated New Year's Eve. He was also a slight, nimble man. Dad always reminded me of a gnome, kinda quiet with a huge toothy grin.

At his wake service, when all the New Year's Eve gang came by to pay their respects to Dad, I heard so many stories about his shenanigans on New Year's Eve. I had heard all the stories before many times, but they still brought a snicker and chuckle to me. The one I heard the most was when he played leap frog with Ralph, his neighbor across the field. These two hard-working farmers acted like frogs and leaped all around the party house. Annie, who was hosting the party that year, was scared to death those two grown men were going to leapfrog down the basement steps as she had an open stairway.

Annie told the story again at Dad's wake, laughing and giggling as she recounted their game of leap frog. It indeed was a tale worth repeating! Her eyes were moist but full of cheer as she thought about Dad and how he loved New Year's Eve! You see, my dad's birthday was on December 31. Every year he celebrated his birthday at the annual New Year's Eve party. Dad never really said too much, but this was one night when he obviously cut loose and enjoyed every minute.

ANITA C. DETERS

So many stories about Dad live on in our family. After a long day's work in the sun, Dad would come into the house, pop open a bottle of beer, pour it in a glass, crack two eggs into it, and slug that mixture down in one big gulp. He did this for the protein, I guess. I heard two of my nephews debate this, but I can attest that I witnessed Dad gulp down that concoction many times.

In his later years, Dad became a bit obsessed with burning brush. I often thought of him as being a pyromaniac. After having to call the fire department several times, Mom established the habit of checking Dad's pockets for matches before he went outside.

Dad walked and partied out of this world in March 2003 at the age of 95, bearing the reputation of being a neighborhood legacy in his own right. The following December on New Year's Eve, my father's birthday, I wrote this poem in memory of Dad.

A GAL GROWING UP GREEN CREEK

Today is my dad's birthday.
Forever 95 is he,
A kind and gentle soul,
But the neighbors did say
That every New Year's Eve
At their legendary Par-Tee
Dad would laugh and shout
And dance all about!!
Happy for you, Dad!
Your big bright teeth and sparkling eyes
Greet me many a night
When mine are shut tight.
See you soon, Dad.
Then, together, we
Will have our own Par-Tee!

Chapter Nine
Confraternity

I grew up in a rural community where everybody I knew was Catholic, and everyone played Pinochle!

For many years, the church had organized the parishioners in confraternity groups. My parents belonged to a group with two other couples. We were all friends and neighbors just down the road from one another, so this confraternity group was really a social outing rather than a lesson in Catholicism.

Once a month on a Saturday evening, three couples would gather at a home of one in the group. They rotated who would host the event. All these couples were Catholic, which meant lots and lots of kids were hauled along to this monthly gathering.

The adults would read aloud out of their catechism book in the living room of the home. It was a round robin kind of reading. But, boy, they read fast, really fast. And discussion? Well, nobody disagreed with what was being discussed. It was, "Yep, yep, you are so right. Yep, yep. That's right!" Bam! And just like that, the reading and discussion of the catechism were over and done, and those smoking hot Pinochle cards were thrown out on the kitchen table.

Now, these serious Pinochle players loved to pound their fist of knuckles hard on the table as they declared, "Trump!!" There was a direct correlation of pounding on the table with the amount of beer consumed.

I believe at times teams were determined by pulling of cards. For example, the three high cards would be on one team, and the three low cards on another. If, by chance, a husband and wife ended up on a team, one would occasionally hear the husband chastise the wife, "Why did you lay that card? Why didn't you lay your ace?" And the other couples would snicker.

There wasn't any gossiping going on during Pinochle. These were no nonsense players. No time to talk about neighbors, crops, or anything else. Their world revolved around meld, tricks, and bids for at least three hours or more.

And the kids? Well, it was like those parents could ignore anything on confraternity night. Kids ran amuck in the house. We yelled and screamed and ran in and out of the house. Nobody cared. The adults had a night out, and, by God, come hell or high water, they were going to enjoy it!

We little girls would look at the board games the host family had to offer and decide which ones we would play. I knew my favorite board game at each house! Frequently, a boy would play with us if he wanted. We all knew each other quite well.

When the weather was pleasant outside, both boys and girls ran in the yard chasing each other round and round. My favorite games outside were Flashlight Tag and Dare Base. My front yard had a long clothesline going through the middle. No worries. Some kid only had to run into that clothesline one time, and they always remembered it was there after that.

Sometimes, the boys would sneak away and go, well, who knows where? When confraternity was at my cousins' house, two of my cousins and I would work ourselves into a frenzy by marching up and down the long, dark, hilly lane chanting,

"Lions and tigers and bears, oh my!" We would yell and scream and run up and down that long hilly lane convinced that lions and tigers and bears were chasing us.

Usually around 11 or 11:30 p.m., the parents had to wake up children who were sleeping in a corner or on a couch or maybe on a bed and invite them to the kitchen table for cake and coke or homemade grape juice.

As time went on and I eventually went to parties as a teenager, guess what was going on and what I was asked to join? That's right! A game of Pinochle. We were bidding, melding, and yelling, "Trump!" Just like our parents and catechism taught us. What goes around comes around!

Chapter Ten
First Grade in Green Creek Elementary School

Although my first year of experience in school was horrendous, for the most part, I enjoyed it. I liked the social aspect of going into a classroom and saying hello to all of my classmates. The beauty of first grade was that I didn't have any judgments about anybody. I liked all of my classmates. Every single one of them. The teacher—not so much.

I attended a small four-room schoolhouse in the country, Green Creek Elementary. There was no air conditioning, so many days in the spring, the windows would be flung wide open and that fragrant country air would waft through the classroom. Across from the schoolhouse, farmers worked in the fields, spreading the manure. I loved that. No kidding. Manure smelled like spring to me.

A GAL GROWING UP GREEN CREEK

Each of the classrooms housed two grade levels. My class ended up with 19 students and the class above me had 12 students. Every other year, my class shared a room with the class below me, and the following year, we combined with the class above me. I do not recall how many students were in the class below me. I know I preferred sharing the space with the class above me because the boys who were a year older than me were cuter than the younger boys, and I liked them more.

However, during my first year of school, my classroom housed only first grade students. I believe this year, 1966, the school district started bussing the eighth grade students into a school about 10 miles away, so the youngest children in the school had this frightening teacher all to ourselves.

Sister Merwyn. Oh my. She was a Catholic nun teaching in a public school. This lady had no business being a teacher, much less a nun. I became a nervous wreck this first year of school. I think everyone of us in that classroom worked hard to protect each other from the scorn of that woman. Before the school day started, we were unsupervised in the classroom. A student would volunteer to stand watch by the window. As soon as the watchman spotted the nun walking down the path to school in her sacred garb, fully equipped with the veil and long, flowing black gown with big sleeves and rosary beads hanging down from the waist, the child would yell out, "She's coming," and we would race to our seats and quickly settle down into silence, an unnatural state for six-year-olds.

I don't remember ever crying at school, but I do recall crying one night, all night long, on my dad's lap. I was upset because of the grades I received on my first report card. My grades were terrible. But the grade that bothered me the most was my "F" for effort. This is how that nun determined my grade for effort: She lined the students up with our backs against the wall with the chalkboard behind us and instructed to hold out our arms straight in front of us with our fingers out straight as well. She then took her grade book and slowly walked down the row of little ones in front of her, scrupulously inspecting our hands. The amount of dirt under our fingernails determined our grade for effort. She made a mark in her book as she inspected our nails and hands. Now, how many of those six-year-old farm kids do you think had clean fingernails?

My mom told me I was having difficulty in school because I was so spoiled. It was an accusation that totally confounded me. Was it my fault that I was spoiled? How did I spoil myself? Somebody please tell me so I could stop doing it!!

Apparently, not only was my effort failing, but so was my reading. I remember being told to stay in at recess and practice reading. That nun also told me to get my brother to teach me to read. I escaped the classroom during recess, ran to the basketball court, and crossed the country road to get to a slab of cement where the older boys shot hoops. This was where I found my brother who was in the seventh grade. I told him that Sr. Merwyn said he was to teach me to read right now. My brother was either scared of Sr. Merwyn or just a really nice brother because he left his group of friends and came with me to teach me how to read during recess.

I wasn't the only one scared of this nun. My mom and dad were too. They were afraid their youngest child would flunk first grade. A plan was put into place. I called it the "Act really, really nice to guilt the nun into passing our daughter" plan. The following is how it went down: One of Mom's many talents was cooking. She definitely knew how to please the palette. She was bound and determined to get this nun on her side through the stomach. Mom invited Sister Merwyn and the two nuns she shared housing with in the small convent, which was beside the church and next to Green Creek Elementary School, for supper on a night during the week. That afternoon, my dad started the routine of milking the cows earlier than usual so he could be dressed in his Sunday best in time for this momentous meal. I came home from school and sat and watched Mom prepare a luscious pot roast and all the side dishes. Mom pulled the dining room table into the middle of the dining room, took out the fancy tablecloth, cloth napkins, and the china. As Mom polished the silverware stored in a wooden box that was only used for special occasions, my anxiety increased. Mom mindfully set the table so all the settings were perfect. Wow! Watching my mom go to the nines on my account made me feel queasy. My stomach began to gurgle. I did not feel well. Dad came in from the barn and put on his Sunday best. Then, Mom put on her Sunday best, and finally I was told to put on my Sunday dress, the one my uncle from Chicago gave to me.

Show time!

The nuns, who had dressed in their full garb with flowing veils, gowns with big sleeves, and rosaries hanging from their waists, entered our house and exchanged pleasantries with my parents. We sat down at the dining room table, and Mom placed the food on the table, country style. We passed the delicious pot roast and the rest of the food around the table.

I sat across from one of those nuns and looked at her as I placed a slice of pot roast in my mouth and started to chew. I chewed. And I chewed. My God, that hunk of meat was getting bigger and bigger, juicier and juicier in my mouth. I looked at that nun, and I could not swallow. I chewed and chewed some more. I tried to swallow again and that hunk of meat would not go down! My throat had closed up tight!

"Anita! Take the meat out of your mouth and put it on your plate!" said my mom. How embarrassing! I pulled that hunk of gooey mess out of my mouth and put it on my plate. My stomach was cramping.

"Anita! Why don't you lie down on your brother's bed!" Mom said to me.

"Oh, thank you!" I just couldn't look at that nun sitting across from me for another second!

I retreated to the bedroom and closed the door. Now, this door normally opened and shut just fine, but the doorknob was unbelievably difficult to turn, especially for a nervous six-year-old girl.

I lay down on the bed and my stomach started to churn. I knew I was in trouble. I jumped up and tried to turn the doorknob so I could run to the bathroom. The knob would not turn. I frantically started pounding on the door. Dad answered my pounding by slapping a hand over my mouth and running with me through the dining room to the bathroom, where I emptied the contents of my stomach.

Later in the evening, the nuns said their goodbyes. I came out of the bedroom just in time to see Mom close the door behind them. She slumped against the door, loudly proclaiming, "I ain't never doing that again!"

Twenty minutes later, just as the family was starting to relax, sitting around staring at the dining room table like it was a battlefield, the phone rang. It was one of those nuns saying she had lost her rosary and would dad please go outside and look for it. Dad took a flashlight and scoured outside the yard and even went down the lane looking for the rosary beads. He came in and shook his head.

The phone rang again. "Oh, never mind. I found my rosary."

Mom and Dad glared at each other.

The next morning, I was called up to Sister Merwyn's desk. "Are you feeling better today?" My God, the plan was already working! It was the first time that nun said anything nice to me and showed a smidgeon of compassion.

The following school year, I entered the second grade classroom for the first time with my dad. Oh my God! There to greet me was the most beautiful, slender young lady I had ever seen. She had flowing brunette hair, and her long, lean legs were covered in silk stockings. She wore a pencil skirt, a beautiful top, and a necklace, and she smelled good too! She had on green velvet heels. Oh, how I loved those heels! Mrs. Kirk would be my second and third grade teacher. Guess what was written in the comment section of my first report card in second grade? In beautiful handwriting, it said, "Anita has great comprehension of what she reads. She has the best vocabulary in the entire classroom."

The plan worked.

Chapter 11
Mrs. Kirk and Bringing Down the House

While my first grade elementary year was less than stellar, my second through seventh grades at Green Creek Elementary steadily improved both academically and especially socially.

Mrs. Kirk, my second and third-grade teacher, was a beautiful young woman. She was blessed with both a love of music and a musical talent. Besides teaching the second and third grade mixed classroom, she also taught music to all the grade levels. I wish I knew more about her musical background, but I do know she passed on the love of music to all of us farm kids! She produced and created vaudeville-like shows that our school performed onstage at the church hall, which was across the parking lot and on the same grounds as our public school. Those were great times! I learned so many vaudeville tunes and Broadway songs that easily pop into my head to this day. Our mothers made simple costumes that did not require a lot of work. I am sure the mothers appreciated that.

The church hall filled to the max on the day or night of the show, and the air was electrified with excitement and anticipation. The performers ranged from first through seventh grade. Mrs. Kirk involved all the students and paid equal attention to everyone. Not one child felt slighted that another was given more time onstage than another.

When performance time arrived, Mrs. Kirk banged out the tunes on the piano, directing and commanding the students with her bobbing head and with the help of an occasional free hand when it was not dancing on the keys. She was a sight to behold as she orchestrated the entire production.

I located a couple of my classmates and my sister from those times, and they, too, had such fond memories of those productions! One of those was Linda Ungrund Schumacher.

"Ooh, I have good memories of those times!" Linda said. "I remember singing and dancing the Charleston to a song called 'Five Foot Two, Eyes of Blue.' I loved that one! I think we also sang and danced to one called 'What Made the Red Man Red?' That sounds like it would be offensive, but I don't think anyone thought about that in the '60s, at least not in Green Creek. I also remember that Mrs. Kirk played the piano for the THS (Teutopolis High School) musicals and would sing the songs with us. I can still recall a lot of the words for songs from *Oklahoma* and *South Pacific*. I remember singing 'I'm Gonna Wash That Man Right Outa My Hair.' Did we perform that one? Seems like we did, but I'm not sure."

The following is the letter I wrote to Mrs. Kirk in August 2024.

> *Dear Mrs. Kirk,*
>
> *I hope this letter finds you happy and healthy!*
>
> *I am your former second and third-grade student from Green Creek. My sister, Dolores, dated your brother, Steve, just a little fun fact to jog your memory of who I am.*
>
> *My sister-in-law has encouraged me for the last few years to write down memories of my childhood. I was hesitant, as I myself do not*

have any children and didn't really know if anybody would really be interested in my stories. However, that encouragement led me to become a member of a writing group where we do, indeed, write life memories and read them aloud to the group.

I have begun to write about my experiences at Green Creek Elementary. Are you aware of how many people remember the great vaudeville shows conducted and produced by you and how much joy you brought to that farming community?

I asked my sister and another classmate if they remembered those plays, and here is the response I received:

"I remember a play that we did where we sang the song, 'I'm Gonna Wash That Man Right Outa of My Hair.' We ran around the stage and ran our fingers through our hair. Another song we did we were Indians, and we trotted around singing, 'Hana Mana Ganda.'"

"I remember singing 'I'm Late, I'm Late For a Very Important Date!' We made top hats with rabbit ears to wear

while we danced. This was from Alice in Wonderland."

I, myself, remember singing "We Are Siamese If You Please" and "Ain't She Sweet." The girls dressed like 1920s flappers with beads, furs, etc. and paraded in front of the stage one by one. My classmate Loretta Buening had a wolf whistle when she did her dance and paraded in front of the stage! What fun! I also remember singing "Oklahoma!"

The Green Creek Hall was filled with laughter, joy, and a strong feeling of community and pride during those performances!!

You then turned the entire experience into a writing assignment the following week. I was in the second grade. We tots were able to relive the entire night of fun entertainment through our writings.

Well, writing these has led me to think that perhaps I could turn my memories into a small book with all sorts of whimsical stories about my life! Dream big, they say!

A GAL GROWING UP GREEN CREEK

I would love to honor you in my writings! I would like to have a short quote or perhaps even a long quote from you in regards to your perspective of these creative productions at Green Creek. The following questions may help you respond to my request, if you choose to do so.

What motivated you to put on these fantastic productions? How did you create these shows? How did the ideas form in your mind? Do you have a favorite show at Green Creek? Do you have a favorite teaching memory from Green Creek Days and, if so, what was it?

Thank you so much! Please reach out to me in any fashion you feel is the most comfortable.

Anita Deters

I waited patiently for Mrs. Kirk's response. I was thrilled to see her letter in my mailbox!!

Anita,

What a delight to hear from you after all these years. Several of my Green

ANITA C. DETERS

Creek students are in the forefront of my memory and you are one of those. Even my husband, Bill, remembers me coming home and saying, "Anita said this" or "Anita wrote this today."

I always wondered what "magic potion" the Green Creek parents used to raise such enthusiastic and affectionate children. You all were a joy to teach.

The vaudeville shows came about from my love of music. I tried to choose songs that the students would most enjoy singing (and acting). What surprised me was the innate musical talent experienced in the Green Creek community. I wondered if it arose from their German heritage — Germany — the land of Bach, Beethoven, and Brahms.

Some of the older boys would give up their softball games and recess to practice singing, and this was voluntary and simply amazing to me.

Anita, I saved some of your essays for many years, but we've moved so many times that I doubt if I can find them. I do have an old cassette tape of one of the G.C. Christmas concerts and I'd like to find a sound specialist to remaster it. If so, I will send a copy to you.

A GAL GROWING UP GREEN CREEK

Some of my favorite memories:

1. *The class lining up next to my desk to tell me something special before formal lessons began.*

2. *The homemade bread waiting in the car when I was ready to leave for the day.*

3. *Driving out to Green Creek and thinking, "Gee! I'm being paid to do something I love!"*

But teaching handwriting would have been my downfall, eh?

I think it's a wonderful idea to turn your stories into a book — Go for it!!

Thanks a million for getting in touch.

Love and blessings, Linda

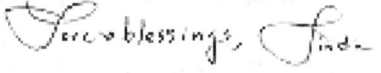

The laughter from the audience at these shows brought joy to every student and parent. Mrs. Kirk was a blessing to our community!

I am not sure how long Mrs. Kirk taught at Green Creek as my class moved on to the next room and the next teacher, Sr. Kathleen. I believe Mrs. Kirk's husband was pursuing higher education in the field of psychology, so they moved on as well. However, Mrs. Kirk was in the area at one time several years later, visiting her mother. My friends Gail, Linda, Barb and Sue and I got wind of this, and we rode our bicycles ten miles into a local town to visit her. She had had her first child not long before that. It was such a delight to see her, and we visited them all afternoon. We reminisced about all the wonderful, happy times at Green Creek Elementary. As my friends and I peddled the ten miles to our homes in Green Creek, the excitement of having visited our second and third-grade filled us.

Recalling these times in my childhood brings me so much happiness but also a tad bit of sadness. I wish for more of those simple times again. I wish every child could experience having that one really special, awesome teacher who makes such a difference in their lives

Chapter 12
Sr. Kathleen Throwing Down!

I spent my fourth and fifth-grade years in school with Sr. Kathleen. The south side of the classroom had windows that faced the blacktopped playground, and the east side looked out on a field farmed by a local farmer. The front of the room, the north side, had blackboards, of course, and the other side of the room led into the hallway.

Sr. Kathleen was a large woman with short blonde hair and wore wire-rimmed glasses. She was one of the first nuns to wear regular street clothes, although she usually chose to dress in a plain brown skirt with a white shirt. She also did not wear a veil except on occasions. She was a local gal who knew our families' lineage and probably a few family secrets, as is common in small communities. She also graduated in the same class as my brother-in-law, Charlie, which immediately put me at an advantage in the classroom. At least in my mind, I was one of her favorites, just as she was a favorite of mine.

Sr. Kathleen was full of laughter and joy and had a huge belly laugh. When something tickled her, she could not contain herself. She would laugh until she gasped for breath. She told stories of her own experiences of growing up on the farm, including one about how she always reacted to eating potatoes. She would get sick to her stomach. Her mother did not believe her when she said the potatoes made her sick. Well, her mother tried to trick her one day by making potato pancakes. Sr. Kathleen ate them, and sure enough, she puked all over. She shared the story to make the point that sometimes mothers just won't believe you until you take extreme measures to prove them wrong or right, whatever the case may be. Sr. Kathleen laughed and giggled as she told us the story about those potato pancakes.

Sr. Kathleen was so relaxed in her demeanor. I loved her! She would lean against the wall and take a cord to the window shade and swing it round and round, and she would break into song. She loved to sing and had a beautiful soprano voice. When I saw the movie *Sister Act*, the nun in that movie with the high-pitched soprano voice, played by Actress Kathy Najimy, reminded me of Sr. Kathleen!

A GAL GROWING UP GREEN CREEK

Sr. Kathleen loved to listen to our farm stories. Actually, it was quite easy to get her off task. Several of the boys figured this out quite early in the school year, so sometimes they would lead Sr. Kathleen astray. She finally figured out that these boys had her number, and she laughed when they tried to get her off topic. She was a great teacher who made learning fun because of her great sense of humor.

As I said, Sr. Kathleen was chill—except for when she wasn't! On occasion, the frustration of being a teacher would overcome her normal, easygoing nature. When she became frustrated, the energy in this large woman exploded with the force of a category four hurricane. As I recall, an unorganized desk frustrated her the most. Seeing a desk that was so messy a student couldn't find the daily assignment or one with papers loosely flying around like a dustbowl really set her off. The frustration of watching a student dig and dig through the mess inside that old desk became just too much for her. More than once, I witnessed her round face turn bright red, and I knew some sort of excitement was about to occur. She would march up to the old timey desk, the kind that was connected to a wooden chair, lift it up singlehandedly, and with a mighty heave-ho would flip that desk upside down, causing a loud thud on the floor. You could tell this was a woman who was used to heavy farm work! The student, usually a certain boy, would just stare in bewilderment at this upside down mess with papers scattered all around. The expression on his face said, "Here we go again."

At times, I looked in awe at this wonder woman exerting her strength, and at other times, I had to stifle a snicker. Today, I understand your frustration. Sr. Kathleen. After teaching special education to adolescents for 38 years, I certainly get it. I also understand what an excellent teacher you were. I thought about you many times throughout my own experiences in the classroom. You were a true way-shower. Thank you!

I contacted her in 2024 and received this wonderful letter in return.

September 11, 2024

Dear Anita,

> *What a pleasant surprise to receive your letter today!*
>
> *Yes, I am at Heartland for some rehab. I retired from Catholic Charities on the last Friday in June. I fell at my sister's house on July 3rd. It took me a couple*

of days and rolling off my bed before I decided to go to the hospital. After a stay of about a week at the hospital, I was transferred to Heartland for some rehab. I am having a difficult time walking, but do not want to have knee surgery at my age. Soon to be 85!

I am happy you that you have such fond memories of Green Creek School. I, too, enjoyed teaching there. The children were well behaved because of the good behavior from their homes. That made school enjoyable for both the teacher and the student. Learning then became fun for all in school. When the children cooperated and got their work done, we could take time to do fun things in the classroom and outside on the playground.

Even after school waiting for the bus, we would play outside. I remember building an igloo one winter. We made the opening big enough so the kids could crawl in and out of the igloo as they played. Father threw some things out of the rectory. We used some old lamps and things to decorate the igloo in the inside. The children made the opening big enough so they could crawl in the inside and play. Sister Barbara Pals and I also played softball with the bigger kids after school. The sixth and seventh-grade boys have a lot of strength from doing all the farm work. One afternoon, one of the boys hit the ball, and it went all the way to the church and broke a window in the sacristy.

We all collected to pay for the new window, teachers and students that were playing.

That same cooperation carried through the school in each classroom. The families disciplined their children well, and this carried on into the school. This helps the children and teachers work well together. We could enjoy each other as we worked and played together in the classroom.

We also had a good music program. Everyone seemed to enjoy singing. Linda, one of the teachers knew music and helped teach the children. It helps when you have someone who knew music to teach the classroom. T-town schools also had music teachers who helped with the outlying schools. It was a great program. It was great teaching in a school where parents taught their children to respect teachers.

It was a blessing to be able to come to Green Creek to teach and to meet all you good people.

I have a great niece and nephew who live in North Carolina. They also love it there.

Thanks for writing. It was good to hear from you.

Sister Kathleen Buescher

Chapter 13
Sister Barbara and Final Days of the Good Life

Sister Barbara was my sixth and seventh-grade teacher. I really liked this wonderful woman just as much as Sr. Kathleen. She and Sr. Kathleen lived alone in a small brick convent across the playground from Green Creek School and down a short driveway from St. Mary's Catholic Church. The two of them were young ladies, perhaps in their mid to late 20s. These were the first nuns in my small farming community to wear street clothes and not to wear a veil. They were both local women from other farming communities ten to twenty miles from Green Creek. Sister Barbara went to high school and perhaps was in the same class as one of my older sisters. Of course, she knew our families. She, too, grew up as a daughter of a dairy farmer and shared her farm story adventures in class.

A GAL GROWING UP GREEN CREEK

One of the stories that Sr. Barbara told us was that when her mom and dad went out to milk the cows, they would lock her and each of her two sisters in separate bedrooms so they would not fight. I don't know what impressed me most about her story. Was it that her farmhouse had doors that actually worked? I mean, they actually closed and opened as desired? Or was it that the farmhouse actually had enough bedrooms for each sister to be contained? My mind immediately went to what that farmhouse looked like and how it was designed. I am sure there was a life lesson to learn in that story, but it totally escaped me. Perhaps the lesson was that sisterhood never changes and will be forever thus. Yep, that sounds right!

Sister Barbara was a great teacher. I liked her and she liked me. One day, my best friend saw a farmer working the field across from the schoolhouse with his John Deere. She stuck her head and hand out the window and gave him a big wave. Sister Barbara said, "Linda, quit that! Get your head back in the classroom!"

Linda turned to me, as I was standing next to her, and said, "You waved to him yesterday, and she didn't say a word. You get by with everything."

I knew what she said was true, or perhaps my friend just didn't have good judgment about when to stick one's head out of the window.

The sixth and seventh-grade classroom had windows on two sides. The interior wall had a blackboard, and the fourth wall had an entrance/exit that led into the hallway. It was a perfect setup for us to be distracted by the wonders of nature, the workings of the farmers, and the beautiful sounds of songbirds and wind rustling the tree branches, limbs, and leaves. I loved my country schoolhouse!

One reason I appreciated Sr. Barbara was that she challenged us. Some days, we would drill math skills for the entire morning and neglect other subjects. We memorized conversion of fractions to decimals and percentages. To this day, I cannot solve a math problem with an unknown without configuring the numbers into a proportion.

A spelling test in Sr. Barbara's class was not a simple matter. When she said the word, the student was expected to not only spell it on paper but also to give the definition. Learning the meaning of each word was part of the spelling assignment.

Sr. Barbara seemed to want to show us off to the school we moved on to as eighth

graders. I do believe she accomplished this task. We students from Green Creek knew our academics, and we could easily keep up and even surpass the students from Teutopolis Junior High, the school we attended as eighth graders. Sr. Barbara challenged us to think a little deeper about our religion and the philosophy of life. I suppose it stands to reason that eventually Sr. Barbara said goodbye to being a nun. I remember her saying, "All the popular songs on the radio are written about love. Don't you believe that love is the most important thing in life?" She made this statement with a grin on her face. Just like Sr. Kathleen, she laughed easily.

Now, it was also obvious that Sr. Barbara was a Tomboy of sorts. She loved playing softball with the boys, and I really think she enjoyed them in the classroom more than the girls. I can't say that I disagree with her. I often thought that myself as a teacher. Girls just have a lot of pent of emotions, and they just deem it necessary to let it all out in many ways. Many ways.

One day, when I was in sixth grade and sharing Sr. Barbara with the seventh grade class, we students decided to play a trick on her. I don't know who initiated this, but it sure was a good idea.

All of us stuffed ourselves into the cloak closet. It was a free-standing closet, more like a bureau with two wide doors in the front. I don't think we planned to have the girls go into one side and the boys into another. We just shoved ourselves into the closet, and somehow the doors stubbornly shut. Sr. Barbara entered the classroom totally dumbfounded. Where were the students? When those doors toppled open, I still remember the flabbergasted look on her face. She quickly broke out into wails of laughter as we tumbled out of the cloak closet.

Sr. Barbara had a friend who dropped out of the convent way before she did. I believe her friend's name was Diane. On occasion, Diane would stop by in the afternoon with her 12 string guitar, walk around our class, and sing, sing, sing. We would spend the afternoon singing. It was a grand time! "Bah da da dee da." "Feeling Groovy" by Paul Simon was rocking in the classroom on those days.

Cold, snowy days were a blast! We threw many a snowball at each other during recess; however, that didn't compare to the thrill and excitement of what waited for us behind the school: an icy snow packed hill!! When the appointed bellringer for the week rang the recess bell, we raced behind the schoolhouse as fast as we could! On our feet, we slid down that hill and jumped over the small creek that ran around at the bottom of the hill. The entire school of students of all ages got in on the action, and it was a blast!! Many a student had to call home asking their mom to bring them fresh clothes because their pants were soaking wet from falling in the creek.

Sr. Barbara would also organize a "Ride Your Bike to School Day." On that day, we took the afternoon off from academics and together, as a class, we rode our bikes through the countryside. The memory of it reminds me of the scene from *Sound of Music* where all the children were laughing and singing. Good times!

During my Green Creek School days, our bus driver was a special character, a local farmer and a great guy. His name was Ed Doedtman. I do believe all my siblings had the same bus driver. Ed had a jovial greeting when each child entered his bus, and he always gave each one of us a gift of a brown sandwich bag filled with peanuts for Christmas.

ANITA C. DETERS

Ed told me once that he had the toughest route of all the bus drivers in the district. I believe it. Our curvy, hilly route to school was much more challenging when it was snowy and icy. Riding that bus could be quite a thrill in the winter, but Ed always delivered us all safely to and from school. Now, I am not saying there weren't a few adventures along the way, such as the bus sliding in the ditch when the roads were ice packed. At times, all the kids became eerily silent when the bus was having difficulty going up a slick hill.

I miss those school days. As I made the transition from Green Creek Elementary to Teutopolis Junior High, a school that was 10 miles down the road, I rode the bus filled with anticipation and nervousness of what school life would offer me. Reflecting on those days, I never felt that sense of togetherness and "one for all" at school ever again. I never felt the compassion and love of teaching as I did from Mrs. Kirk, Sr. Kathleen, and Sr. Barbara. It was good to grow up in Green Creek. Matter of fact, it was more than good—it was great!!

My country education eventually led me to Teutopolis High School. Teutopolis, which means "City of Teutons" or Germans, was the name of the small town where the school was and is located. According to Wikipedia, it is the only town with this name in the United States. The name of the high school mascot was and is the Wooden Shoes. At one time, a maker of Wooden Shoes lived in Teutopolis. Whenever I want to put a giggle in my day, I stomp around the house chanting, "Stomp 'Em! Stomp 'Em!," as this was our battle cry on the basketball court. Just imagine a gymnasium filled with hundreds of fans, yelling "Stomp Em!" Then, when the tension had built into a fury, the fans would stomp their feet on the wooden bleachers! Oh, man! It was the sound of thunder times ten!

One of my favorite cheers which put the spotlight on the town's German heritage went like this: "Sauerkraut and pig's feet, that's what we eat! Bulldogs! Bulldogs! Gonna get beat!" Then the thunderous stomping would begin! The Bulldogs were our archrivals.

I had a bird's eye view of all the basketball games and the thunderation because I was a member of the band. We sat collectively above the gym floor. We would play the school's theme song and give out blasts of "Charge!!" with our instruments! That was the scene of many weekends while attending high school.

ANITA C. DETERS

Way back when the high school team was first organized in 1935, the coach at that time, John Harold Griffin, named the mascot. He decided to call the mascot the Wooden Shoes to honor George Deymann, a local woodworker who carved them. That coach from long ago happened to be the father of one of my favorite teachers, Mrs. Kirk. How 'bout them apples? Or should I say shoes?

I had a small preview of Teutopolis Junior High before I actually made the transition with my classmates. A small group of us, four, I believe, were in the band since fifth grade. An instructor drove out to Green Creek Elementary once a week to give us four a lesson. After we reached seventh grade, our parents drove us once a week to and from Teutopolis Junior High so we could play with the band and receive lessons with the entire group.

I played the cornet but dreamed of the band instructor switching me to a trumpet once I entered Teutopolis Junior High. I loved my cornet and practiced scales on it every night. I raced through those scales. With my tongue tapping the roof of my mouth, I could play those scales in sixteenth time! I bought a songbook for trumpets from the local music store and had old ones used by my older siblings. I played that cornet for many hours in my brother's bedroom while he was helping Dad milk the cows. Now, I was good but was quite intimidated once a week as we walked into the junior high band room filled with fellow musicians who were strangers to us. To make matters worse, I could hear the boys snicker at me and make fun of my size. I had always been fat, but I don't think I thought of myself as fat until those days when the boys made snarky comments under their breath. I felt even more anxious after the instructor placed me to sit second chair! I had to walk in front of those strangers and take a place of honor as they moved over one chair to allow space for me. Those boys became good friends of mine eventually, but the memory of enduring the weekly band lessons is engraved in my mind.

One of our parents would pick us up after an hour and drive us back to Green Creek, where the bus would deliver us home. I wish I could remember the silly conversations as we returned to our comfort zone. I know we each dreaded those weekly band lessons.

My aspiration of being placed on a trumpet never came to fruition. I was given the dreaded

French horn to play once I entered high school. While I love the majestic, rich sound of the French horn and can easily detect it when I go to the symphony, I never managed to master the technique like I did with the cornet. I never practiced it. I so wanted to play the trumpet! If I had to do it over, I would have talked to the band instructor and expressed my desire. Another life lesson learned: speak up for yourself because you are worth it!

As previously mentioned, the junior high boys got pleasure from making snide comments about my size. Because of my own experiences, I always had a soft place in my heart for overweight girls in my classroom. My heart honestly ached for obese girls, as I knew firsthand how difficult it was to become comfortable in your skin as a teenager. On the other hand, my own personal experience led me to educate young male adolescents to be aware of the feelings of others and, more importantly, to give girls the respect they deserve. Adolescence can be a messy time of learning to accept your self-worth, no matter what your outer being looks like. Challenges in junior high and high school will be forever thus.

A GAL GROWING UP GREEN CREEK

It's still the same old story,
The fight for love and glory…
As time goes by.

Written by Herman Hupfeld sung by Carly Simon

Chapter 14
After 4:00 P.M.

When the school bus dropped us off by the big oak tree at the end of our quarter mile dusty lane, I always felt a sense of relief. The loudness of the school bus in the afternoon was sometimes a little too much for my nerves, and I would end my day with a huge headache. Seeing the old oak tree approaching as the bus slowed down told me it was time to get out of my seat and slowly walk up the aisle to say goodbye to the stressors of the day.

As we slowly meandered down the long and dusty lane towards home, my sister and I could reflect about the day at school—who said what to whom and why it was said. We would share our achievements and disappointments. Also on this walk, we would hear the afternoon freight train, which was a quarter mile from our lane and easily seen across the fields, whizzing by on the tracks. It was all part of the routine after 4:00 p.m. that I found comforting.

Once we completed our leisurely walk down the lane, we entered the white framed farmhouse, sat down at the kitchen table, scattered our book bags on the floor or across a chair, and then enjoyed a yummy snack. Once in a great while, Mom made a something special—chocolate pudding! As we ate, we looked at the *Effingham Daily News*. I religiously read the Ann Landers advice column, which was where I learned most of my life lessons, the comics that I often wondered why I didn't find really all that funny, and the section that showed what movies were playing at the local theater. After this ritual, I went up the stairs to my bedroom, changed into my barn clothes, descended, and took a slow walk to the barn to do my evening chores.

My chores consisted of washing and assembling the milkers, feeding, watering, and bucketing the young calves, pouring feed into the stalls for the cows, bedding the manger for the young calves, and sometimes pitching a bit of silage. The rhythmic pumping of the milking machine was steadfast and relaxing. After the chores, I would visit the calves and tell them about my day, singing to them sometimes. I loved how the young calves would suck on my fingers. Their long tongues were as rough as sandpaper and the slobber from the calf's mouth would be all over my hand. I would go in and out of the milking parlor, lost in my imagination. Many times I would have a staring contest with a cow as she was being milked. I never won.

The barn cats were nasty looking with snot coming out of their noses and eyes and another sort of nastiness coming out of their rear end. They would scatter quickly as soon as they saw a human approach their cluster. I wondered what they were discussing and thinking? The cats hovered around my dad when he poured warm milk straight out of the milking container into their pans. They loved the creamy milk. Those ugly, snarly looking cats were just part of the barn landscape.

In the winter, I often hung out at the barn way past the time when my sister left the house to do her thing. I would practice writing cursive backwards on the ice frosted windows and run around outside to see how pretty my handwriting was, admiring my backwards flourishing penmanship. Eventually, I moseyed down the trail from the barn to the house with the temperature freezing, the sky dark blue, stars twinkling, and the moon shining brightly. I felt so peaceful. Those hours after 4:00 p.m. were a time for reflection, a time to breathe in fresh air and move at an unhurried pace. The walk in the evening was especially enchanting as I would gaze at the stars and moon. I embraced the joy of a simple life after 4:00 p.m.

A few days in the autumn, after getting off the school bus, our chore was to walk the cornfields and pick up the corn cobs the combine had missed. This was an okay job but not particularly my favorite thing to do. On the other hand, my eyes glistened with anticipation when Dad hitched up the grader to the tractor. My sister and I knew we would soon jump on that grader to add a little weight to help smooth out the potholes and prepare the lane for the long winter. That was a blast! Up and down the lane, we stood on the grader, just grinning. Living on a farm has those unexpected delights! A perfect way to add a little excitement to the end of a long school day.

The memory of grading the lane fills my mind with delight even now. There was another activity that holds a special place in my heart because I shared it with Dad. We would go to the Labor Day picnic in Sigel, Illinois, where an annual tractor pull was held. Noise from the tractors gearing up and dust filled the air along with the excitement of the men who just knew their tractor would win the prize for pulling the heaviest weight. At this old-time tractor pull, they used the step-on method where people stood in a fixed position and stepped on the drag as the tractor pulled it. The more people, the more weight, which was how they determined which tractor would win. I remember standing next to Dad as he grabbed my hand. Together, we jumped on that drag and rode it with all the other men. It was so exciting to me! Thinking of my dad jumping on to add weight is actually quite funny since he was built like a nimble gnome! Seeing Dad's big toothy grin as he grabbed my hand before we jumped on the drag still makes me break into a huge grin. It warmed my heart for my dad to grasp my hand and lift my arm, and the rest of my weight would follow. I stood next to him and looked up at him with my big brown eyes and admired his big white toothy grin as he gazed down at me. He was a 60-year-old man with a young daughter, and this old man was loving it! So was I!

  I think of my quiet, nimble, gnome-like dad with a big toothy grin every last day of the year because his birthday was on December 31.

A GAL GROWING UP GREEN CREEK

I wrote this poem many years after Dad said goodbye to the Earth plane, and I was reminiscing about him once again.

Happy Birthday!

Thinking of my dad today

He was really special in his own way.

One hot summer afternoon, when I was feeling kinda sad about

Being in a place I really did not want to be,

I sat down on the swing in the front yard next to my very old dad.

"Dad," I said, not expecting any reply,

"I like the pinks and purples and blues. I miss those colors of the coast. I really do. I miss the salt water too."

And he responded to my surprise, "Oh, Anita," and he slowly raised his arm up in front of him as he painted the scenario: "I like the greens, the tans, and all the shades of brown. I like how they make me feel. I like the Earth. That is what I like."

I slowly turned my head to him in awe and thought.

"Wow! He gets it! He gets me! Who knew?!"

ANITA C. DETERS

Dad lived to be 95. He really did love this earth! Now, when I walk along the trail in the woods, I always think of my dad as I inspect the trees and the leaves. My dad knew the name of all these. Dad, I have grown to really love the Earth! I miss you!

So if you knew G'pa Deters, hug a tree today.
He would like that too.

Chapter 15
Awk and Not

On our kitchen wall hung a trivet that said, "Ach Don't Talk So Dumb." To me, this trivet represented my German heritage. My mom said frequently, "Ach, don't talk so dumb!" Many times, she affectionately added "dumbass" to the end of this phrase. We kids really didn't pay much attention to Mom adding "dumbass." It was just who she was, and many times she said it in a way that made me snicker. The grandkids especially loved to get Mom fired up and have her explode with an affectionate "Dumbass!"

Now, our family said "ach" a lot! It actually was pronounced more like "awk" with a guttural sound from the back of the throat—a true sound that gave away any chance of trying to hide our German Heritage.

Awk was said when one was frustrated. If I couldn't figure out a math problem, a loud "awk" would relieve any headache. If I couldn't find something, you might hear me say, "Awk, where in the hell is it?" Among a family with lots of kids and adults, the sound of "awk" was heard a lot! When Mom was especially frustrated with one of us, she would be a bit more emphatic, shouting, "Awk, you damn dumbass!" As I mentioned previously, Mom could cuss like a sailor when she was agitate school that said "not" so much that his fellow classmates called him "Notty Not." I looked at Mom in disbelief when she told me that story because, honestly, I couldn't believe anybody said "not" more than she did!

Now, in my community, people who used many "awks" and "nots" were sometimes referred to as talking "Dutchy" as my Dad would say. Sometimes, Mom and Dad would refer to somebody and say under their breath, "Oh, they talk so Dutchy!"

Now, our entire family was filled with "awk" and "not" sayers! When I left my German community to go to college, my Dutchy talk became a bit of a problem. My new friends would ask, "Why do you always say, "Not?" I was on the road to becoming a teacher, so students in my practicum would say, "Why do you say 'awk'?" "What does that mean?" I worked really hard to break myself of the habit of talking with awks and nots. I never fully stopped using either word. I occasionally say "not," but I must admit, the "awk" was extremely difficult to break. Now that I am retired, I am not so conscientious about saying "awk" and I just let it fly. I must admit it feels good to return to my roots to express my frustration!

Another expression used in my family, "go to town," has nothing to do with German heritage. We said that because we lived on the farm, and going to town could be a big deal. When I was a little girl, Mom might say, "Put on your good clothes after dinner because we are going to town."

This meant we were going shopping for groceries or something at the feed store, etc. I didn't realize how embedded that phrase was in my psyche until years later when my students teased and poked fun at me when I said something like, "Oh, don't worry about that. I will pick up some paper for you when I go to town." Oh my, how they hooted and laughed. I was teaching in a small city, so my students had no idea why I would say "go to town." They would jeer and say, "What do you mean you have to go to town?" Well, it was a teachable moment, and I would segue into a story about growing up in the country. My students always enjoyed those exaggerated tales, and I enjoyed sharing about growing up on a farm in the Midwest.

"Ach, don't talk so dumb" certainly reminds me of my mom. As she reached her late octogenarian and early nonagenarian years, another phrase she said frequently was "That's right!" Mom was quite smart and clever. She was full of pride and did not want anyone to ever think she was the least bit confused, so when she wasn't sure about something, she would trick you into giving her the correct answer. For example, Mom might say, "What is the name of the farmer across the field?" I would give her the answer, and Mom would say, full of expression like she was the host on a game show, "That's right!" She made it seem that I was the one who didn't know the answer, and she was rewarding me for responding correctly. More than once, my niece Angela was around when this occurred, and we gave each other a side glance and grin. Angela occasionally ends her correspondence to me with "That's right!," which makes me laugh and think about Mom.

Shortly after Mom's funeral, I returned to my home in Raleigh, North Carolina. One Saturday afternoon, I was sitting outside on a bench at an upscale shopping area, listening to the piped in music and thinking pleasant thoughts about Mom. Did I ever get a huge chuckle when a big fancy car drove slowly by with the license plate that said, "That's Right." Well, hello, Mom! Thank you for your spiritual visit!

Chapter 16
Front Yard Follies

Walking the barrel was one of those simple activities that my sister and I did hours on end during the summer. I don't recollect any of our friends having a 55-gallon drum in their front yards. No, walking the barrel was unique only to us. When Dad emptied one of those big oil drums, he threw the barrel in the front yard for us to play on. We would put the barrel on its side and walk forwards and backwards on it. As our talent for this activity improved, we started to run on the barrel. We were always barefoot too. Having bare toes made it so much easier to grip the barrel. Our yard had a slight hill, so we found it a bit of a challenge to walk that barrel forward and then backwards up that incline. Also, a clothesline ran all along our yard, so we learned quickly to duck our heads to avoid an injury. We would walk the barrel by ourselves or sometimes together. It was so much fun! We never tired of it. The only way I could have made this more of an achievement would have been if I had played my cornet while walking the barrel! What a simple activity that brought so many giggles and happy memories.

Our front yard was a feel good place and certainly a source of ruckus and howling laughter. My sister and I would play bean toss, which some today call cornhole, many a game of croquet, and badminton using the clothesline as the net if we didn't want to bother setting up the net. We swung on a tire swing and a simple board swing. Oh, so much fun! We used cushions from an old, worn-out couch for bases when we played ball. We mostly tripped over them or jumped on them to make our landing on the base exaggerated. "So there! I made it to the base!"

My sister Evelyn and I ran like stallions in the front yard when a storm was approaching. We loved the feeling of being recharged and rejuvenated by those negative ions. After dashing around in the front yard like a couple of fools, we always played Captain and the Ship, a game that involved taking a bike and turning it upside down on the front porch. The wheels of the bike suddenly turned into a helm, and the pedals transformed into another mechanism that we would fiddle with on our make-believe ship. We stared out into our "ocean," a sea of green, as we panicked and yelled out orders to our imaginary shipmates. In our minds, we were in the middle of the ocean during a serious storm! We jumped on the concrete and brick short wall on our porch so we could peer out into the eye of the storm and make predictions of the rough sailing. Our imaginations were fired up! Thank goodness we had a mom who wasn't afraid of storms and let us run wild. As the bright lightning surrounded us, we guided our ship to landfall. We never tired of this make-believe scenario. We loved feeling the impending rapture of a storm, if only a made up one!

My sister Evelyn and I brought the technique of riding a bike to a whole new level. My brother still laughs about this as he remembers our countless contortions as we got on the bike. I obviously have difficulty describing how we did it, but we spent many an afternoon perfecting this circus act. Evelyn would sit on the seat, I would perch on the handlebars facing her, and I would pedal or try to. We attempted other methods of pedaling the bike in a unique fashion. Sometimes Evelyn sat on the seat backwards and pedaled.

We called it "riding the bike backwards." This was never an entirely successful endeavor, but we took great pride in accomplishing this trick and pedaling a few feet or even a few yards. More gratifying were the many laughs we had trying this! Evelyn also had a unicycle that she actually became quite proficient at riding, which is hard to imagine, considering she had to practice on a gravel lane. I, on the other hand, had no interest in keeping my balance on one wheel.

Shenanigans in Grandma Schabbing's Yard

Grandma Schabbing was a grandmother to one of my girlfriends in the neighborhood. All the kids in the area referred to her as Grandma Schabbing. I would ride my bike to the mulberry tree on the corner of Grandma Schabbing's property and enjoy eating mulberries. My friends and I called this spot "Schabbing's Corner." On occasion, a bunch of us girls in the neighborhood met on the side of Grandma Schabbing's house, where there was a gravel roundabout of sorts before you got to the barn. We played softball there, but this anecdote has absolutely nothing to do with that. It has to do with being thirsty.

One afternoon, I was over at Grandma Schabbing's yard playing with her granddaughter. My cousin Marilyn was there too. Being little girls, we ran into the house occasionally to get a drink of water on a hot summer day. Marilyn went into Grandma Schabbing's house, grabbed the first glass of water she saw, and slugged it down. Donna exclaimed, "You didn't just drink the water in that glass, did you?"

"Yeah," said Marilyn. "Why?"

"That is the glass of water Grandma always soaks her teeth in."

I am still laughing 55 years later.

Barnyard Buffoonery

Inside the barn up in the loft, away from household chores, our imaginations ran wild. Our cousin Kevin taught Evelyn the technique of building tunnels throughout the hayloft using bales. She showed me the hole where the entrance to the tunnel was, and we crawled through. It immediately became dark but not pitch black, and the sweet scent of hay filled our nostrils. I knew why cows loved eating these greens, because it actually smelled good. If I were a cow, I thought hay would be quite tasty. Evelyn usually designed these tunnels so they led into a space big enough to spread out just a little and relax. That was Evelyn's hideaway. I actually was a tad bit afraid of crawling through the tunnels as I imagined them collapsing on top of me and suffocating me. Not a pleasant way to go if I must say so! Now, Dad didn't always appreciate the tunnels. He would be walking around pitching out bales of hay when suddenly one leg or foot would fall through the bales. That's right. Dad had found one of the passageways to the tunnel. Oops! The tunnels gave us adventure, and many evenings after feeding the calves, we climbed up to the hayloft and crawled around for a short time in the tunnels. Sometimes, we would find a litter of kittens that had just been born. Other times, we might come across a litter of mice pups. Lots of action going on in those tunnels!!

In addition to being a creative architect, my sister was a performing celebrity, as was I. She and I put on many theatrical plays in the barn loft. We hopped around from bale to bale like jackrabbits, playing and rehearsing our roles with enthusiasm. Many girlfriends and cousins performed with us. We all won Grammy awards for our performances in the hayloft!

ANITA C. DETERS

Comments from My Cousin

Every summer, I looked forward to a visit from our cousins who lived in Chicago. It was a special treat when my cousins Sharon and Linda stayed an entire week! I had playmates for the entire week, and Mom gave us chores to do together.

I was surprised and touched when I asked Sharon if she had any memories from those farm days. "Oh, Anita, I have so many special memories from those days—gathering the eggs, watching your mom swing the neck of the hen so we would have fried chicken for dinner! Actually, it was then I learned that chickens aren't bought at the grocery store. And your mom's peach pies! I was always fascinated watching your mom make noodles. She would roll out the dough and then take a sharp knife and hurriedly cut the dough into strips!"

Sharon also talked about putting on plays in the hayloft and laughed out loud as she recalled my mom referring to Dad as "You ole fart!"

We chuckled together as she recalled my dad saying the prayers over the meal. He prayed so quickly that nobody ever knew what was being said. My nieces and nephews would ask, "What language does Grandpa use to say the prayers?"

As a matter of fact, saying the prayers became a sport of sorts for us at the dinner table. We used to time each other to see who could say them the fastest! Our eyes stared at the kitchen clock's second hand to keep score.

Sharon's heartfelt response made me laugh and feel warm all over, knowing that my mom and dad and our country lifestyle had affected her too!

Chapter 17
December Delights

The first of December marked the day when my sister and I began the count. No, not the countdown to Christmas Day but the count of our stair steps. I cannot tell you how many times we practiced tiptoeing down those slick, waxed wooden stairs in our old farmhouse. Our parents' bedroom was below those steps, and we did not want to wake them or anybody else as we made our early morning descent to see what Santa had brought us! We practiced tiptoeing on those steps over and over in our bare feet. We knew there were 17 steps and exactly which ones creaked and moaned as we placed our feet on them. If we decided a step was too loud, we stretched our legs over and skipped it. The night before Santa arrived, we snuck flashlights into our bed so we could make this slick, treacherous journey in the spotlight.

A GAL GROWING UP GREEN CREEK

I am surprised we always arrived under the Christmas tree with fits of glee and no broken bones!

As a side bar, my mom took great pride in those wooden steps. She waxed and polished them at least once a year. It seemed to me that she always took me to town to buy new Sunday shoes the day after performing this chore. You can imagine what happens when a happy little girl puts on those shiny patent leather shoes for the first time along with her Sunday dress to go to church. She skips from her bedroom to the top of the steps and then boom—all the way down! It was a bumpy descent on my butt down those 17 newly waxed and polished steps. It happened every time. I often wondered if Mom intentionally waxed those steps the day before she bought my new Sunday shoes. I still am wondering.

Since our farm community was rich in German heritage, we celebrated St. Nicholas Day. I knew St. Nick would visit my family on the evening of December 6. St. Nick had a different technique to mark his arrival for each family in the community. During this special evening, my family would watch television. I would take my usual position lying on the floor in front of the TV. That evening we would watch with one ear tuned in, listening for a loud "thud" at our back door. Once we heard that thud, we hurried to the door to find a big bag of specialty nuts that we only got to enjoy during the Christmas season.

Because my farm community was steeped in German heritage, we would sing "Old Tannenbaum" at the end of the Christmas service. The only time I heard Dad sing out loud with a vibrant voice in church was when the congregation sang "Old Tannenbaum" and "How Great Thou Art." Dad was proud of his German lineage. To this day, both songs bring sweet tears to my eyes with warm memories of my dad.

Chapter 18
Travels

For the longest time, the only place my parents traveled to was church. Now, that could be quite the adventure for the entire family riding in the black Chevy. I learned quickly that there were two spots to sit that I did not want in the black Chevy. My main goal was to avoid the door in the backseat behind Mom. This door did not always shut tight and would sometimes fly open. I heard those dreaded words, "Hold the door shut, Anita," only one time, and that was enough for me. I was so afraid that door would fly open and I would get thrown out into a cornfield. After arriving safely in the church parking lot, I entered the church, genuflected, and dutifully said prayers of gratitude.

Never again.

The second position was in the front seat between Dad and Mom. While Dad would drive, Mom would take the opportunity to clean out your ears all the way to church. Mom would dig into her purse, find a handkerchief, cover her pointer finger with the cloth, and proceed to dig into your ear canal. Squirming and yelling a few cuss words under one's breath didn't deter her. It was not a pleasant experience. I learned to judge the perfect time to head for the black Chevy on Sunday mornings and get a choice of seats in the back.

Now, the trip to church in the winter months could be both harrowing and exciting. Besides having a door that sometimes flew open, we traveled over roads covered with ice and snow. Our dutchy language called it "slick ice." Going up and down Green Creek hill on the way to church could be quite a challenge on the ice.

When the country roads were slick, the cars lined up, as one by one as each driver attempted to get their vehicle up the icy hill on our route to church. The men helped guide and push the cars up the hill. I felt frightened yet excited as one by one the cars made it up the hill covered in snow and ice.

The first real get away vacation Mom and Dad took was with my sister Evelyn and me to Branson, Missouri. I am guessing my brother was old enough by then to manage the farm and milking by himself, but I am not sure.

Dad was quite proficient in knowing his way around on the interstate, even though interstates were new to him. After milking the cows, he spent many a night sitting by the kitchen table studying road maps.

We made it to Branson just fine; however, once we arrived in a cheap motel, Mom pulled an electric skillet from her suitcase and plugged it in, hoping to fry up something for us to eat for supper. She plugged it in and after a few minutes, *kaboom*! All the lights not only in our bedroom but in the entire motel blew out! We were all frightened. Mom quickly hid that electric skillet and out the door we went. We ate out in a restaurant after all. What did we do in Branson? I have no idea. Nothing compared with the excitement of blowing out the fuses in that motel!

Chapter 19
No Other Than My Mother

I entered a contest sponsored by *The Effingham Daily News* to write a story about your mother, explaining why she should be "Mother of the Year." The winner would receive a diamond necklace. Oh, how I wanted that necklace. When I put my pen to paper, the words came out as a poem, not a story, so I did not win. Instead, I was interviewed by the paper because so many women could relate to this poem. If you are a daughter, perhaps you will relate to it too.

No Other Than My Mother

I look in the mirror
And face what was once my worst fear
It is clear have turned into no other than my mother!
It is clear my mother should be
Mother of the year, can't you see?
She had to survive, there was not compromise,

A GAL GROWING UP GREEN CREEK

She had to face her fate, with no debate
She birthed six girls—all replicas of her!
Who could have endured?
No other than my mother.
Now slow to move but still quick to shout,
She's really quite a runabout.
She's got style, she's got grace
Who's got that smile on her face?
No other than my mother.
Well, there she goes again
Independent and classy
Now who's being sassy?
Oh brother, guess what?
It's my mother!
My vote's for you because you are the special one,
But I look into the mirror and get confused:
Are you me, or am I you?
Oh well, it's hard to tell.
I vote for you because you are second to none.
You are
No other than my mother,
Marcella Deters.

Chapter 20

My tales have come to an end.
It is time for me to put down my pen.

My mind has taken me on quite a journey—
Whew!! I am surprised I wasn't taken out on a gurney!

Lessons are learned by twists and turns.
Hold on tight.
Not all is in sight!

Take a step back
And then look at the view.
What you thought to be facts
Aren't always true.

Learn to see the clues
Do what you do
Put on your crown
And be you!

A GAL GROWING UP GREEN CREEK

Throw in some laughs,
Some cries and tears.
We created this path.
Now skip along the years.

The Universe guides us,
Though you may not know it.
Let your light shine,
And you'll be fine.

To your own self be true,
And you will capture the prize.
Spirit will guide you.
Just enjoy this slippery slide, because time does indeed fly by.

Anita C. Deters

When the day becomes the night and the sky becomes the
sea. When the clock strikes heavy and there's no time for tea;
and in our darkest hour, before my final rhyme,
she will come back to Wonderland
and turn back the hands of time.

—Alice in Wonderland
by Lewis Carroll

About the Author

Anita C. Deters grew up in a small German farming community outside of Effingham, Illinois. The wind blew through her hair as she rode her bike up and down the hills. It was a time filled with laughter and joy. This carefree spirit remained nestled inside her as she enjoyed teaching for 38 years. Upon retirement, Anita's creative side exploded as she made a plethora of rag dolls, painted a multitude of garden poles and sang with joy in her heart as she strummed the ukulele with any one of her many hats on her head. Anita presently makes her home in Raleigh, North Carolina.

www.ingramcontent.com/pod-product-compliance
Lightning Source LLC
Chambersburg PA
CBHW070108080526
44586CB00013B/1229